Juvenile Firesetting: An Exploratory Analysis

by
Michael Lawrence Slavkin

ISBN: 1-58112-108-3

DISSERTATION.COM

USA • 2000

Juvenile Firesetting: An Exploratory Analysis

Copyright © 2000 Michael Lawrence Slavkin
All rights reserved.

Dissertation.com
USA • 2000

ISBN: 1-58112-108-3

www.dissertation.com/library/1121083a.htm

JUVENILE FIRESETTERS: AN EXPLORATORY ANALYSIS

Michael Lawrence Slavkin, M.A.(R), L.P.C., N.C.C.

Submitted to the faculty of the School of Education
in partial fulfillment of the requirements
for the degree
Doctor of Philosophy
in the Department of Counseling and Educational Psychology
Indiana University

June 2000

Announcement Page

Announcing the
Final Examination of
Michael Lawrence Slavkin
for the
Degree of Doctor or Philosophy in the Department of
Counseling and Educational Psychology
Friday June 30, 2000 3:00 p.m.
School of Education, Room 4112

Dissertation: Juvenile Firesetting: An Exploratory Analysis

This study had two primary purposes. First, this study assessed the psychometric properties of the FEMA forms (Fineman,1997a, 1997b, 1997c), inventories used by the Federal Emergency Management Agency (FEMA) to assess recidivism in juveniles. Second, this study initiated preliminary analyses between variables that (1) contributed to the identification of a typology of firesetters, (2) predicted the severity of fires set by juveniles, and (3) predicted the likelihood of recidivistic behaviors in juvenile firesetters. This study was performed with a limited range of exploratory predictors; including age, sex, delinquency, social skills, and psychopathology. It was expected that certain individual and environmental characteristics would relate to varying levels of damage caused by the fire, and the presence or absence of recidivistic behaviors. However, individual characteristics (delinquency, social skills, and psychopathology) were better predictors of recidivism, the magnitude of fire damage and the typology of firesetter.

Outline of Studies   Educational Career

Major: Educational Psychology   M.A. - Saint Louis University - 1996
Minor: Counseling Psychology   B.A. - DePauw University - 1993

Committee in Charge

Professor Gary Ingersoll   Chairperson   856-8321   Educational Psychology
Professor Myrtle M. Scott   Committee Member 856-8313   Educational Psychology
Professor Marianne H. Mitchell   Committee Member 856-8335   Counseling Psychology
Asst. Professor Anne D. Stright Committee Member 856-8316   Educational Psychology

Approved: _____

Gary Ingersoll, Ph.D. - Chairperson

Acceptance Page

Accepted by the Graduate Faculty, Indiana University, in partial fulfillment of the requirements for the degree of Doctor of Philosophy.

Gary Ingersoll, Ph.D. - Chairperson

Doctoral Committee

Myrtle M. Scott, Ph.D. - Committee Member

Marianne H. Mitchell, Ed.D. - Committee Member

Anne Dopkins Stright, Ph.D. - Committee Member

Date of Oral Examination - June 30, 2000

Acknowledgements Page

I wanted to take the opportunity to thank several people. Thanks to all of my colleagues in the program (Stephanie Bales, Carin Neitzel, Cathy Garza Sears, and Bryce Fox) who have pushed me forward and kept me going, especially at those times that I was most frustrated. As the guinea pig of the dissertation experience, I am thankful that I had the chance to work with you and learn from you all. Thanks also for reviewing earlier drafts of this paper!

Special thanks to Dr. Marianne H. Mitchell and Dr. Anne Dopkins Stright for serving on my coursework committee and for mentoring me from the earliest days of the program. Also, special thanks to Dr. Myrtle Scott, who has been instrumental in organizing my thoughts about development and individual-environmental interactions. Thanks for always believing more in me than I did in myself.

Dr. Gary Ingersoll deserves special mention as my dissertation chair, and the person who has read this paper and organized its ideas into a coherent body of work. Thanks for taking a chance on an unusual project, and for allowing me to become an upstart in a field needing significant support! Also, thanks to Barbara Spurlin, the director of MCAIN and my original mentor in the field of juvenile firesetters – who would have guessed that the persistent phone calls WOULD have made the difference?

Finally, I must thank my wife and parents, who stuck by me during four years of hard work. Their financial and emotional support has made all the difference in the world! This paper is dedicated to the memory of Dorothy Slavkin, a scholar and learned woman in her own right. Thank you for always believing in my abilities, for teaching me to write and think, and for making me aware of the need for confidence and quality in life.

Abstract

This study had two primary purposes. First, this study assessed the psychometric properties of the Federal Emergency Management Agency (FEMA) questionnaires used to record juvenile firesetting events (Fineman, 1997a, 1997b, 1997c). Second, this study initiated preliminary analyses that (1) contributed to the identification of a typology of firesetters, (2) account for variance in the severity of fires set by juveniles, and (3) predicted the likelihood of recidivistic behaviors in juvenile firesetters. Predictors were restricted to a limited set of exploratory variables; including age, sex, delinquency, pathology, and social skills. However, individual characteristics (delinquency, social skills, and psychopathology) were better predictors of recidivism, the magnitude of fire damage and the typology of firesetter.

Juvenile Firesetters: An Exploratory Analysis 6

TABLE OF CONTENTS

Chapter One: Introduction 13
Purpose and Rationale. 13
    Scope of the Problem 13
    Purpose of the Study 14
        Site selected for the evaluations 15
    Conceptual Framework of Study 15
Hypotheses of the Study. 18
Limitations of the Study 19
Summary 19

Chapter Two: Review of the Literature 21
Overview 21
Juvenile Firesetting 21
Psychoanalytic Orientation 22
    The ego triad 23
Individual Characteristics 24
    Aggression 24
    Delinquency 26
        Deviance and vandalism. 27
    Externalization of Emotions 28
    Attention seeking behavior 29
Environmental Issues 29
Environmental Proximal Controls for Firesetting 30
    Family problems 30
    Economic Stressors 33
Environmental Distal Controls of Firesetting. 34
    School problems 34
    Peer problems 34
Firesetting across Early Childhood and Adolescence . . . 35
Firesetting in Young Children (Ages 3 to 6 years) . . . 35
    Fire-safety skills 37
Firesetting in Children (Ages 7 to 10 Years) 37
    Early learning experiences 38
Firesetting in Early Adolescents (Ages 11 to 14 Years) . . 38
Firesetting in Late Adolescents (Ages 15 to 18 Years) . . 39
Typology of Juvenile Firesetters 40
Curiosity Firesetter 41
Accidental Firesetter 41
The "Cry for Help" Firesetter 42
Delinquent Firesetter 42
Severely Disturbed Firesetter 43

Cognitively Impaired Firesetter 45
Sociocultural Firesetter 46
Summary 47

Chapter Three: Methodology 48
Introduction 48
Data Gathering Protocol 48
Firesetting Events 48
Fire Site Evaluation of Event 49
Referral to Fire Stop Program 49
    Fire Stop Program staff 50
    Fire Stop Program curriculum 50
Fire Stop Program Interview 51
    Family Fire Risk Interview Form 52
    Juvenile Fire Risk Interview Form 53
    Parent Fire Risk Questionnaire. 53
Status of MCAIN Data Files 54
Creating a Data File 55
    Decisions regarding the data 55
    Missing data 56
    Miscoded data. 56
Measures 56
Demographic Factors 56
    Age groups 56
    Gender 57
    Family configuration 57
    Race 57
    Socioeconomic status 57
    School 58
Predictor Variables 58
Individual Characteristics 58
    An affinity for aggression 58
    An affinity for delinquency 59
    Externalization of emotions 60
Environmental Characteristics 61
Proximal Controls 61
    Family problems 61
Distal Controls 63
    School problems 63
    Peer problems 63
Other Independent Variables Examined 64
    Enuresis 64
    Cruelty to Animals 65

Dependent Variables 65
    Type of Firesetter 65
    Recidivism 65
    Magnitude of Fire Damage 65
Participants 66

Chapter Four: Analysis of Federal Emergency Management Forms . 68
Introduction 68
FEMA's Fire Risk Interview Forms (Fineman, 1997a, 1997b, 1997c) . 68
    Construction of the inventories 69
FEMA's (1997a) Family Fire Risk Interview Form . . . 70
Administration and Scoring 70
Psychometric Qualities of the Family Fire Risk Interview Form Scale. . 70
    Health history scale 71
    Family structure issues. 71
    Peer issues 72
    School issues 72
    Behavior issues 72
    Fire history 73
    Presence of crisis or trauma 73
    Characteristics of firestart 74
    General observations 74
Test-Retest Reliability 75
The Revised Form of the Family Fire Risk Inventory. . . . 76
FEMA's (1997b) Juvenile Fire Risk Interview Form . . . 78
Administration and Scoring 79
Psychometric Properties of the Juvenile Fire Risk Interview Form Scales . 79
    School issues 79
    Peer issues 79
    Behavior issues. 80
    Family structure issues. 80
    Presence of crisis or trauma 81
    Fire history 81
    Characteristics of firestart 82
Test-Retest Reliability. 83
The Revised Form of the Juvenile Fire Risk Inventory. . . 84
FEMA's (1997c) Parent Fire Risk Questionnaire . . . 84
Administration and Scoring 86
Psychometric Properties of the Parent Fire Risk Questionnaire Scales. . 86
    School issues 86
    Health history issues 86
    Peer issues 87
    Behavior issues. 87

Somatic and psychiatric issues.	87
Fire history	88
Family structure issues.	88
General pathology	88
Test-Retest Reliability.	89
Conclusions for FEMA Fire Risk Interview Forms	90
Chapter Five: Results	92
Hypotheses of the Study	92
Examination of Scales.	93
Exploratory Factor Analysis	94
Jessor's Theory Revisited: Pathology, Delinquency, and Social skills	95
Factor one: Pathology.	95
Factor two: Delinquency	96
Factor three: Social skills.	96
Revised Hypotheses under Investigation	97
Reduction in Firesetter Types and Categories of Race.	99
Preliminary Analyses Regarding the Types of Firesetters	99
Enuresis and Recidivistic Firesetting.	106
Predictors of Magnitude of Fire Damages	107
Regression Analysis	108
Age	108
Type of firesetter	108
Parent fire risk factor scores	108
Magnitude of fire damage.	108
Error Variance.	109
Normality	109
Homoscedasticity/Homogeneity of Variance	109
Linearity	109
Results for the linear regression.	109
Cross validation	110
Predictors of Recidivism	111
Regression Analysis	111
Results for the linear regression.	112
Cross validation	112
Predictors of the Typology of the Juvenile Firesetter.	113
Results for the linear regression: Curiosity firesetters.	114
Cross validation	114
Results for the linear regression: Accidental firesetters.	115
Cross validation	115
Results for the linear regression: Cry for help firesetters.	116
Cross validation	117
Results for the linear regression: Delinquent firesetters.	117

    Cross validation 118
    Results for the linear regression: Severely disturbed firesetters. .118
    Cross Validation 119
Developmental Trends in Juvenile Firesetting. 120
    Pathology 120
    Social skills 122
    Delinquency 124

Chapter Six: Discussion 127
Psychometric Properties of the FEMA Forms 127
Enuresis and Recidivistic Firesetting 128
Predictors of Magnitude of Fire Damage 129
Predictors of Recidivism 131
Predictors of the Typology of the Juvenile Firesetter 132
    Curiosity firesetter 132
    Accidental firesetter 133
    Cry for help firesetter 133
    Delinquent firesetter 134
    Severely disturbed firesetter 135
Dependent Variables Under Investigation 137
Firesetting across Early Cildhood and Adolescence 137
Types of Juvenile Firesetters 139
Implications of Findings on Future Research 140
Future Examinations of Juvenile Firesetting 141
    Deviance and violence in youth. 142
    Delinquency, firesetting, and leisure time 142
    Descriptors surrounding firesetting 142
    Parental influence on social skills. 143
    School problems and firesetting. 143
    Identity problems and firesetting 143
    Sociocultural theory and firesetting 144
Summary 144

References 145

Table 1: Typology of Firesetters 44
Table 2: Questions identified for Affinity for Aggression scale. . . 59
Table 3: Questions identified on Affinity for Delinquency scale. . . 60
Table 4: Questions identified on Externalization of Emotions scale. . 61
Table 5: Questions identified on Family problems scale . . . 62
Table 6: Questions identified on School problems scale. . . . 63
Table 7: Questions identified on Peer Problems scale . . . 64
Table 8: Review of Sample with Gender x Age Group . . . 66
Table 9: Means, Standard Deviations, and Level of Skew for Variables . 67
Table 10: Reliability Estimates for the Family Fire Risk Interview Form . 75
Table 11: Items Chosen for the Revised Version of FEMA FFRIT. . 77
Table 12: Reliability Estimates for the Juvenile Fire Risk Interview Form . 83
Table 13: Items Chosen for the Revised Version of FEMA JFRIT . . 85
Table 14: Reliability Estimates for the Parent Fire Risk Questionnaire . 89
Table 15: Reliability Estimates for Individual and Environmental Scales . 93
Table 16: Related factor loadings for the FEMA PFRQ . . . 98
Table 17: Crosstabulation between types and sex of firesetters . .100
Table 18: Crosstabulation between types and age of firesetters . .102
Table 19: Crosstabulation between types and race of firesetters . .105
Table 20: Coefficients Entered in Regression Model to Predict the
   Magnitude of Fire Damage by Juveniles 110
Table 21: Coefficients Entered in Regression Model to Predict
   Recidivistic Juvenile Firesetting 112
Table 22: Coefficients Entered in Regression Model to Predict
   Curiosity Firesetters 114
Table 23: Coefficients Entered in Regression Model to Predict
   Accidental Firesetters 115
Table 24: Coefficients Entered in Regression Model to Predict
   Cry for Help Firesetters 116
Table 25: Coefficients Entered in Regression Model to Predict
   Delinquent Firesetters 117
Table 26: Coefficients Entered in Regression Model to Predict
   Severely Disturbed Firesetters 119
Table 27: Analysis of variance symmetry of pathology in juvenile
   firesetters by sex, race, age group, and type of firesetter . .122
Table 28: Analysis of variance symmetry of social skills in juvenile
   firesetters by sex, race, age group, and type of firesetter . .124
Table 29: Analysis of variance symmetry of delinquency in juvenile
   firesetters by sex, race, age group, and type of firesetter . .126

Figure 1: Crosstabulation between types of firesetters and sex of firesetters .101
Figure 2: Crosstabulation between types of firesetters and age of firesetters .103
Figure 3: Crosstabulation between types of firesetters and race of firesetters .106

Appendix A	.157
Appendix B	.158
Appendix C	.159
Appendix D	.160
Appendix E	.162
Appendix F	.166
Abstract	.212

CHAPTER ONE
INTRODUCTION

Purpose and Rationale

Jackie and Jordan, four- and five-year-olds growing up in downtown Indianapolis, were left alone to play in their bedroom on a Friday evening after dinner. Thirty minutes later, the smell of smoke and the screaming of children filled the house. Jackie and Jordan's parents, downstairs at the time of the fire, were only able to save their youngest children as they escaped their burning home. Within 10 minutes, everything they owned was destroyed and Jackie and Jordan were dead, the result of playing with a lighter the children took from their father.

Scope of the Problem

Each year, fires set by juveniles account for a large portion of fire-related public property damage and deaths. Fires set by children and adolescents are more likely than any other household disaster to result in death (National Fire Protection Association, 1999). In 1998, it was estimated that fires set by children and juveniles resulted in 6,215 American deaths, another 30,800 injuries, and two billion dollars in property damage (National Fire Protection Association, 1999). During the same timeframe in Marion County, Indiana alone, juveniles set 81 fires; resulting in $650,000 in damage, 21 critical injuries, 6 civilian fatalities, and 2 fire fighter fatalities (State Emergency Management Agency, 1999).

Despite the costs and impact of juvenile firesetting, it remains a little studied area of research. What limited research that does exist is dominated by a psychodynamic perspective. In her seminal work, Yarnell (1940) attributed maladaptive firesetting to a conflicted ego identity, sexual dysfunction during the process of maturation, and the outcome of sexual abuse. Few investigations of firesetting have been conducted using an alternative theoretical stance.

Research on juvenile firesetting also has been hampered by methodological and statistical limitations. Examinations of juvenile firesetting have been based on data from case studies or from research using projective instruments, which are of limited generalizability. These studies project an image of juvenile firesetters as a uniform group, not acknowledging wide intragroup differences among the forms of firesetting and the magnitude of fire damage. Studies of juvenile firesetting typically depend upon data drawn from hospitalized or institutionalized samples. The reliance on samples of hospitalized or institutionalized firesetting youths reinforces the stereotyped perception that most juvenile firesetters are psychologically disturbed. Both of these methodological constraints affect the ways in which youthful firesetters are viewed by professionals in fire service, mental health, and education.

Purpose of the Study

The purpose of this study was to investigate individual and environmental factors that contribute to the form and risk of continuation of firesetting in juveniles. The researcher utilized data taken from a county-based dataset on child and adolescent firesetters. The Marion County Arson Investigation Network (MCAIN) is a countywide database compiled by fire professionals who investigate incidents of firesetting within Indianapolis and Marion County, Indiana.

The database is a subset of the Federal Emergency Management Agency's (FEMA) database on juvenile firesetters. By acquiring information on firesetters from MCAIN, the researcher sought to acquire a more representative sample of firesetting juveniles. MCAIN's use of a series of standardized measures to collect information from both the firesetter and family members (Fineman, 1997a, 1997b, 1997c) is an improvement over previous research, which has focused solely on case study or interview data.

<u>Site selected for the evaluations</u>. Data from MCAIN were gathered as part of a national data program under the aegis of FEMA, the national organization responsible for collecting information on firesetting. Though geographically restricted, the data are assumed to offer broader generality. The State of Indiana's death rate per capita as a result of fire ranks at the median by state for the United States, with 15.8 people being killed per million citizens (National Fire Protection Association, 1999).

MCAIN has collected information on all fires reported in the Indianapolis area and Marion County since 1993. As such, the dataset does not suffer the limits of previous studies that have relied on hospitalized or institutionalized samples. However, the MCAIN sample of firesetters is not without its constraints; inclusion occurs only when the identity of the juvenile firesetter is determined. As with any intact data set, analysis is restricted to only those data points collected.

Data from this dataset provided information on juveniles who have set fires in the MCAIN geographic area during the previous 6 years (1994-1999). The researcher used the following as dependent variables: (1) the magnitude of fire damage (based in dollar amount lost due to fire), (2) the presence of recidivism, and (3) the typology of firesetters as functions of individual characteristics (e.g. - aggression, delinquency, externalization of emotions) and environmental circumstances (e.g. – family problems, school problems, peer problems).

<u>Conceptual Framework of Study</u>

Juvenile firesetting remains an understudied area. The last significant review by Kolko (1985) concluded that the individual's personality characteristics, in addition to the juvenile firesetter's environment, related to firesetting and recidivism. In the years since the Kolko (1985) review, limited additional research has occurred (also see Barnett & Spitzer, 1994).

Most attention to firesetting has been subsumed within broader categories of delinquency and aggression in children (Kazdin, 1990). However, no separate review of firesetting from a developmental framework has been performed. It is believed that juvenile firesetting, much like other forms of delinquency and aggression in juveniles, can be explained as examples of problem behaviors.

Firesetting can be classified as one of many examples of problem behavior that has been identified in juveniles. In proposing his problem-behavior theory (Jessor, 1987; Jessor & Jessor, 1984), Richard Jessor asserts that most juvenile problem behaviors can be explained by an examination of the particular characteristics and experiences of juveniles (individual characteristics) within the contexts defined by a larger society or culture (environmental characteristics). In order for social scientists to understand a problem behavior, individual factors and environmental factors must be examined, in addition to the attributes of the situation in which the problem behavior takes place (Jessor, 1981; Jessor & Jessor, 1973).

Jessor, Graves, Hanson, & Jessor (1968) identified three systems of psychosocial influence that lead to problem behaviors in juveniles: the individual system, the environment system, and the behavioral system. Jessor (1987) states

> Within each of the three systems, the explanatory variables generate a dynamic state called proneness, which specifies the likelihood of occurrence of normative transgression or problem behavior. Problem behavior is defined as behavior that departs from the norms – both social and legal – of the larger society; it is behavior that is socially disapproved by institutions of authority and that tends to elicit some form of social control response whether mild reproof, social rejection, or even incarceration (Jessor, 1987, p. 332).

Proneness is thought to be synonymous with the propensity to engage in problem behavior. While proneness can be identified as being related to specific individual, environmental, or behavioral events; it is generally reviewed as a global, psychosocial risk factor (Jessor et al., 1968).

Jessor and Jessor (1973, 1977) also assert that problem behavior theory emphasizes the dynamic and systemic interaction between individuals and their environments. Like Lewin's (1951) field theory, problem behavior theory is an interactional model that asserts causal priority cannot be attributed solely to either individual or environmental characteristics. To explain a problem behavior as complex as firesetting, both individual and environmental predictors must be examined simultaneously (Magnusson & Endler, 1977).

Individual characteristics are defined as social and cognitive experiences that occur throughout development, and often reflect social meanings, values, expectations, and orientations toward self and others (Jessor, 1987). Individual characteristics that were examined in the present study include an affinity toward aggression, an affinity toward delinquency, and an externalization of emotions. Environmental characteristics are defined as supports, controls, models and expectations of others that are thought to be meaningful phenomena to juveniles (Jessor, 1987). Environmental controls that were examined in the present study include family problems, school problems, and peer problems.

In previous studies of deviancy, marijuana use, drug use, cigarette smoking, sexual intercourse, and alcohol use problem-behavior theory has accounted for approximately 50 to 60 percent of the variance in composite measures of juveniles' problem behaviors (Donovan & Jessor, 1978; Donovan & Jessor, 1985; Jessor, 1987; Jessor et al, 1968; Jessor, Chase, &

Donovan, 1980; Jessor & Jessor, 1984; Rachal, Guess, Hubbard, Maistro, Cavanaugh, Waddell, & Benrud, 1980). For the purposes of the present research study, the researcher identified factors that were thought to influence firesetting in youth. Exploration of these factors and their relations to the maladaptive behavior patterns of these children and adolescents has implications for better recognizing the developmental patterns that lead to juvenile firesetting.

The present study's emphasis on developmental factors that contribute to the initiation or continuation of juvenile firesetting has implications for the ways in which parents, educators, and counselors work with these youth. By acquiring information on firesetters from the MCAIN datafile, the researcher sought to acquire a more representative perspective of juvenile firesetters. It is hoped that using this dataset will assist with the community's understanding of this problem, as well as improve the programming designed to intervene on behalf of these youth.

Hypotheses of the Study

This study investigated the following hypotheses:

1. The presence of enuresis and cruelty to animals in juvenile firesetters will be related to recidivistic firesetting.
2. The magnitude of fire damage will be predicted by individual and environmental factors, with environmental factors being found to be better predictors.
3. The presence of recidivism will be predicted by individual and environmental factors, with individual factors being found to be better predictors.
4. The typology of the juvenile firesetter will be predicted by individual and environmental factors, with environmental factors being found to be better predictors.
5. A developmental pattern will be identified with juvenile firesetters, with early

childhood and child firesetters being predicted more with environmental factors, while adolescent and young adulthood firesetters being predicted more with individual factors.

6. Firesetting in young children is more likely to result in greater destructiveness to property than the firesetting of any other age group.

Limitations of the Study

Limitations of the study were:

1. No observational data of firesetters' families, schools, or peer environments were collected. Moreover, no observational data were collected on juveniles' level of aggression, delinquency, or externalization of emotions.
2. The MCAIN database is not the entire universe of Marion County's firesetters.
3. Data only were collected on those referred to MCAIN's Fire Stop program.
4. Data were limited in that they are constrained by only those questions asked by MCAIN.

Summary

Juvenile firesetters represent a population of significant social concern; current understanding of this population is limited. This study explored the relationships among individual and environmental variables and firesetting during early childhood and adolescence. The theoretical context that describes this population is closely aligned with Jessor and Jessor's problem behavior theory (Jessor & Jessor, 1984). The significance of the problem as a characteristic of atypical development also is reviewed.

Chapter 2 contains a review of the psychological, sociological, and criminological literature on firesetting in juveniles. Related fields of literature are discussed, as are the results of studies relating firesetting in youth with the literature on aggression and family context.

Chapter 3 delineates the character of the existing data set and strategies for analysis, as well as the use of quantitative methodology in the study. The relationship between the research questions and the problem is established. The data collection sample is described, as is the instrumentation that was used.

Chapter 4 provides a discussion of the reliability and validity of the Federal Emergency Management Agency instruments (Fineman, 1997a, 1997b, 1997c), forms used by the federal government since 1984, but which have never been investigated as to their effectiveness in identifying firesetting.

Chapter 5 provides a general discussion of the results of the study, including the first identified review of firesetting from a developmental context.

Chapter 6 summarizes these results and relates them to the present state of the field. This chapter also includes a discussion of future directions that research needs to take in looking at juvenile firesetting.

CHAPTER 2
REVIEW OF THE LITERATURE

Overview

The purpose of this chapter is to review the existing literature on juvenile firesetters, focusing first on the individual characteristics related to firesetting in youth, and second on the environmental contexts that can be used to predict juvenile firesetting. This chapter also examines the contribution of individual and environmental characteristics to (1) the magnitude of damage caused by fire, (2) the presence of firesetting recidivism, and (3) the typology of juvenile firesetters.

Juvenile Firesetting

Juvenile firesetters are typically defined as children or adolescents that engage in firesetting. Beyond its tautological character, such a definition implies a singularity about firesetting in children and adolescents. It is more appropriate to distinguish among types of juvenile firesetters. Previous classifications of juvenile firesetters have been based on individual characteristics (e.g., personal motives, physical problems, interpersonal ineffectiveness/skills deficits, and covert antisocial behavior excesses) as well as environmental characteristics (e.g., limited supervision and monitoring, parental distance and uninvolvement, parental pathology and limitations, and presence of crisis or trauma.) (Kolko & Kazdin, 1992). An adequate understanding of juvenile firesetting is contingent upon the simultaneous examination of individual and environmental factors (Barnett, Richter, Sigmund, & Spitzer, 1997).

Psychoanalytic Orientation

When examining motivating forces behind juvenile firesetting, many reviews have relied on a psychoanalytic orientation (Kaufman, Heims, & Reiser, 1961; Lester, 1975; Rothstein, 1963; Yarnell, 1940). Those writings are largely based upon Freud's (1932) assertion that firesetting in youth is a regressive retreat to "primitive man's" desire to gain power and control over nature. In Civilization and its Discontents, Freud (1930) states:

> In man's struggles to gain power over the tyranny of nature, his acquisition of power over fire was the most important. It is as if primitive man had had the impulse when he came in contact with fire, to gratify an infantile pleasure in respect of it and put it out with a stream of urine . . . Putting out fire by urinating . . . therefore represents a sexual act with a man, an enjoyment of masculine potency in homosexual rivalry. Whoever was the first to deny himself this pleasure and spare the fire was able to take it with him and break it into his own service. By curbing the fire of his own sexual passion he was able to take fire as a force of nature . . . It is remarkable how regular analytic findings testify to the close connection between the ideas of ambition, fire, and urethral eroticism (Freud, 1930, p. 50).

Since this original publication in 1930, Freud's perception of the youthful firesetter has guided the firesetting literature with the perception that juvenile firesetting is an ego-oriented conflict that seeks removal of man's sublimation to nature's rule.

In her seminal work on juvenile firesetters, Yarnell (1940) examined 60 cases of juvenile firesetters from patients admitted to the psychiatric division of Bellevue Hospital New York. Yarnell (1940) asserted that firesetting in juveniles is the result of (1) castration fears, (2) enuresis, and (3) the influence of the mother figure in the life of the child.

Yarnell speculated that youth who set fires do so in order to gain power over adults. She also emphasized the neglectful nature of the relationships between mothers and their sons. Yarnell examined juveniles' relationships with fathers as they related to professional issues, such as for children whose fathers are fire professionals. The author supported Freud's view that these juvenile firesetters have difficulty with enuresis and cruelty to animals and to others (Yarnell, 1940).

The ego triad. Yarnell proposed an ego triad among juvenile firesetters that linked the co-occurrence of enuresis, cruelty to animals and others, and firesetting in youth. Reports of the comorbidity of these behaviors and its predictive power in identifying adult criminal behavior has been verified in a number of studies performed following Yarnell (Lester, 1975; Prentky & Carter, 1984; Robbins & Robbins, 1967; Rothstein, 1963; Wax & Haddox, 1974).

It is not surprising that these three behaviors were identified simultaneously in juveniles who set fires; the studies that validated the triad were performed using institutionalized samples. Moreover, these reports were based on case study reviews and data extrapolated from projective instruments (Kaufman et al., 1961; Lester, 1975; Macht & Mack, 1968; Quinsey, Chaplin, & Upfold, 1989; Rothstein, 1963).

Juvenile firesetters are more likely than other groups of juveniles to have been cruel to children or animals as well as have difficulties with enuresis (Quinsey, Chaplin, & Upfold, 1989; Sakheim & Osborn, 1999; Sakheim, Osborn, & Abrams, 1991; Saunders & Awad, 1991), although the predictiveness of these factors is limited (Blumberg, 1981; Heath, Gayton, & Hardesty, 1976; Showers & Pickrell, 1987). Justice, Justice, and Kraft (1974) questioned whether the ego triad is an adequate system of identification in predicting violent behavior in adulthood. The authors assert that the ego triad largely is identified as occurring simultaneously with factors that may be better predictors of violent adult behaviors. The presence of individual characteristics, such as fighting, temper tantrums, school problems, and truancy, in combination with environmental factors, such as interpersonal difficulties appear to be better warning signs of adult violence or criminality (Justice et al., 1974). Although the ego triad serves as a poor indicator of antisocial and violent behavior (Heath et al., 1976; Prentsky & Carter, 1984; Wax & Haddox, 1974), members of the psychological community continue to emphasize its validity (Heller, Ehrlich, & Lester, 1984).

Individual Characteristics

Factors within firesetters are used to predict and explain the maladaptive patterns of firesetting (Showers & Pickrell, 1987). Individual characteristics examined in this study include a tendency toward aggression, levels of delinquency, and the externalization of emotions through the use of fire.

Aggression

Aggression in youth is not typically seen as a developmental difficulty until it is evidenced in tandem with behaviors of noncompliance and disruption. Early childhood noncompliance and aggression have been identified as indicators of lifelong difficulty with aggression if interventions are not initiated (Carey, 1997; DeSalvatore & Hornstein, 1991). Firesetting has been closely related to antisocial behaviors in youth (Fineman, 1995; Raines & Foy, 1994). Patterson (1982) asserts that firesetting may occur at the extreme of a continuum of antisocial symptomology that progresses from high-rate, overt symptoms, such as disobedience; to low-rate covert symptoms, such as lying, stealing, and vandalism.

Achenbach (1966) theorized that internalization or externalization of behaviors impacts aggression in children and adolescents. Children who internalize emotions are more likely to report depressive or somatic symptoms while children who externalize emotions through their behaviors show a higher level of acting out against others. Firesetting according to Achenbach's classification system reflects an externalizing of emotions.

Rice and Harris (1996) found that among adolescent male firesetters at a maximum-security psychiatric hospital, that one-third of firesetters also had been reported to engage in other aggressive and violent offenses. Also, Kolko and Kazdin (1991) reported a relationship between early childhood firesetting, heightened aggression, and social skills deficits (also see Forehand, Wierson, Frame, Kemptom, & Armistead, 1991).

Burgess and Akers (1966) state that aberrant criminal behavior is a shaped response to cultural and environmental stimuli. Social learning theory asserts that individuals learn how to behave and respond to environmental stimulation by watching others' behavior and by imagining themselves performing similar behaviors (Bandura, 1977; Neilsen, Harrington, Sack, & Iatham, 1985).

Loeber and Stouthamer-Loeber (1998) reviewed the literature on juvenile aggression and violent behavior and identified a number of age-related patterns in its development. The authors found that there is a discontinuous relationship between early childhood aggression and aggression in early adulthood. The authors also found that not all forms of violence have their origins in early childhood. The authors suggest that violent behaviors and aggressive attitudes need to be examined as they relate to the age of onset, time involved in the duration of the aggressive attitude, and age of the reduction of aggression (Loeber & Stouthamer-Loeber, 1998; also see Loeber, Keenan, & Zhang, 1997). It would follow then that the best model to describe aggressive behaviors would be a triple-pathway model that integrates an overt pathway, a covert pathway, and an authority conflict pathway (that are integrated along a developmental trajectory).

Delinquency

Firesetting research has neglected the connections between juvenile recidivism and patterns of delinquency. Junger and Wiegersma (1995) examined the relationship between mild deviance and involvement in accidents, as well as common correlates of the two. Mild deviance was described in terms of gambling, drinking, smoking, soft-drug use, shoplifting, and vandalism, which are common examples of delinquent behavior.

Results show that mild deviance was related most closely with leisure time activities. Youth with low involvement with passive leisure time activities (e.g., often hanging out with friends, going out with friends, or having a job at 13 or 15 years of age) were less likely to engage in mildly deviant activities (Junger & Wiegersma, 1995). These results are similar to that previously identified by Kolko and Kazdin (1988), which indicated that some firesetters engage in firesetting and destructive behaviors as a result of boredom.

Heaven (1994) found that adolescents that were self-described as delinquent were more likely to engage in violent, sensation-seeking, and aggressive behaviors. These teens reported that their families set up weak boundaries for their behaviors. Eyesenck (1994) views such delinquent behaviors as a natural extension of the desire to seek pleasure and avoid pain, in that most offending juveniles who consistently act in sensation seeking ways are less likely to have built up conditioned responses against such "hedonistic tendencies" (Eyesenck, 1994).

Raine, Reynolds, Venables, Mednick, & Farrington (1998) found that children who were destructive and fearless at age 3 years were more likely to become aggressive and delinquent by age 11 years. Larger body size at age 3 years, but not at 11 years of age characterizes aggressive children (Raine et al., 1998).

Deviance and vandalism. Firesetting has long been considered a form of social deviance in youth (Fineman, 1995). Loeber, DeLamatre, Keenan, & Zhang (1998) assert that deviance can be classified as behaviors that are bothersome to adult caregivers (e.g., highly stubborn behavior, lying, truancy, running away from home) or that inflict harm or property loss on others (e.g., physical aggression, vandalism, theft, violent acts). Kazdin (1990) posited that deviance in early childhood is most closely connected with a diagnosis of conduct disorder (see also Barnett et al., 1997; Repo & Virkkunen, 1997). Early childhood deviance is often revealed in disobedience and unmanageability early in early childhood, if not during pre-school ages (ages 2-5 years).

Daderman and af-Klintenberg (1997) found that juveniles who had been arrested for vandalism had a greater likelihood of being criminal before the age of 15 years, and that most were violent offenders, with almost three-fourths having difficulties with substance abuse. These results correspond with many of the results previously-discussed about aggression, with vandals scoring higher on measures of impulsivity, sensation seeking, and low conformity (Hanson, MacKay, Atkinson, & Staley, 1994).

While 10% of juveniles who are arrested are juvenile firesetters, juvenile firesetters are more likely to be involved in a greater proportion of arrests overall when compared to other arrested juveniles. Firesetters also engage in property destruction and crimes of physical aggression, such as forcible rape (11%), nonviolent sexual offenses (18%), vandalism (19%), and arson (35%) (Williams, 1998). Kolko and Kazdin (1991, 1994) found that adolescent firesetters have higher levels of antisocial behaviors, higher levels of aggression, and are more likely to connect their deviance with covert aggressive expressions when compared with other firesetters.

Goldstein (1996, 1997) believes that vandalism is best reviewed if intraindividual qualities and the environment are examined. As emphasis has turned to more dramatic expressions of aggression, such as fights, assaults, involvement in gangs, and juvenile use of guns; less attention has been placed on less damaging expressions of aggression, such as graffiti and the destruction that comes from juvenile firesetting (Goldstein, 1996).

Cohen (1989) suggests that investigators examine the factors that lead to society's belief that misbehavior relates to deviance and vandalism. Cohen also asserts that motivation is critical in understanding whether a behavior is commonplace rule breaking or vandalism (Cohen, 1989).

Externalization of Emotions

Results indicate that firesetters tend to have conduct problems, such as disobedience and aggressiveness. It is thought that these maladaptive behaviors are juvenile firesetters' primary method for expressing feelings (Forehand et al., 1991; Thomas & Grimes, 1994). Sakheim, Vidgor, Gordon, and Helprin (1985) also found that firesetters had feelings of anger and resentment over parental rejection, and that such feelings largely were expressed covertly through the use of fire. Externalization of emotions for firesetters is accomplished through the use of fire (Sakheim & Osborn, 1999; Thomas & Grimes, 1994).

Children and adolescents who set fires are identified as having poor social awareness and limited ability or opportunity to express themselves. Juvenile firesetters also are easily angered by insults or humiliations, resulting symptoms that resemble attentional deficits. Kolko (1983) found that early childhood firesetters can be characterized as having multiple behavior problems with few internalizing behaviors, such as depression, but many externalizing behaviors, such as rule breaking, aggression, and destruction. Prior examinations of youth firesetting have emphasized the intraindividual dynamics of children, focusing on the problem by relating it to some internal dysfunction that is either genetic or due to a developmental anomaly (Raines & Foy, 1994). However, the firesetting of these juveniles are most likely the result of environmental influences and limited coping skills (Kolko & Kazdin, 1991).

The current study is based on the premise that aberrant behavior, such as firesetting, occurs when children and adolescents suffer from weak or nonexistent bonds to family or society. The limited ability to interact with family, schools, or peers reduces their chances to learn or engage in traditional methods of emotional expression. That, in turn, leads them to behave in socially unacceptable ways.

Attention-seeking behavior. Though largely ignored by research, attention-seeking behaviors are often a factor involved in juvenile firesetting, as is the desire to get a reaction from parents, authorities and emergency services (Schwartzman, Stambaugh, & Kimball, 1994). Most attention-seeking behavior is classified according to the functions of the behavior. Behaviors classified as attention-seeking would include any behavior performed to provoke others, or any negative action performed in order to attain a tangible reinforcer (Lee & Miltenberger, 1996). Although no studies of attention-seeking behavior in juvenile firesetters have been performed, Luby, Reich, and Earls (1995) and Taylor and Carr (1994) found that children involved in neglectful environments were more likely than children who were in traditional supervision settings to engage in attention-seeking behavior.

Environmental Issues

Further consideration needs to be made of the environmental characteristics and interindividual dynamics that relate to the firesetting of juveniles. Environmental characteristics are defined as supports, controls, models and expectations of others that are thought to be meaningful phenomena to the juvenile (Jessor, 1987). Achenbach's (1966) theory is similar to the tentative risk model originally identified by Kolko & Kazdin, in that both subscribe to an interactive relationship between individual characteristics and environmental factors (1986a; 1986b).

Jessor & Jessor (1973) and Jessor (1981) have argued that variability in problem behaviors stems largely from differences in perceptions of environmental characteristics. Proximal controls refer to the prevalence or models and supports for problem behavior. Environmental proximal controls that were examined in the present study include family problems. Environmental distal controls that were examined in the present study include school problems and peer problems.

Environmental Proximal Controls for Firesetting

Kolko and Kazdin (1994) assert that parent and family characteristics promote firesetting and a continuation of patterns of firesetting. Moderate youth firesetting has been associated with limited family sociability, whereas recidivism has been associated with lax discipline, family conflict, limited parental acceptance, and family affiliation (Kolko & Kazdin, 1994). Parental influences such as limited supervision and monitoring, early learning experiences and cues with fire, parental distance and uninvolvement, and parental pathology have been identified as predictors of juvenile firesetting (Kolko & Kazdin, 1985, 1986a, 1991).

Family problems. Kolko and Kazdin (1991) have identified correlates between parental maladaptive behaviors and child maladaptive behaviors (Kolko & Kazdin, 1988). However, few professionals examine such environmental conditions when working with firesetters (Federal Emergency Management Agency, 1988, 1995, 1996). In reviewing the relations between family dynamics and juvenile firesetting, Squires and Busuttil (1995) determined that a significant number of house fires were directly related to the activities of adults in the home. Poor supervision and a lax child-care environment were found to be better predictors of recidivism in children than intraindividual factors (also see Kolko & Kazdin, 1988; Showers & Pickrell, 1987). Moreover, adults spent a limited amount of time keeping track of incendiaries in the home, which increased juvenile access and ability to set fires (Squires & Busuttil, 1995).

Firesetting in young children has been identified as being largely the result of a neglectful family environment (Gaynor & Hatcher, 1987). Macht & Mack (1968) have asserted that the family environment of the early childhood firesetter is likely to be chaotic and limited in nurturing behaviors. Patterson (1982) believes that early childhood firesetters show the beginnings of antisocial behaviors, and that the externalization of emotions through firesetting resembles adolescents who are victims of abuse and neglect. As a result of these theories, unwanted and unacceptable early childhood behaviors are thought to be largely the result of a neglectful and abusive home environments.

Neglectful behavioral patterns of parents and caregivers may place children at a higher risk for playing with matches, as well as destroying property through the use of fire. Kolko and Kazdin (1994) found that access to incendiaries, lack of adolescent remorse, and lack of parental consequences for negative behavior were associated with follow-up recidivism (multiple incidence of firesetting). Furthermore, Squires and Busuttil (1995) assert that the fatality rate connected with juvenile firesetting could be significantly reduced if abusive and neglectful behavior or uninvolvement with children was reduced and parental support was increased.

Some firesetting juveniles engage in destructive behaviors as a result of family context.

Psychosocial maladjustment has been related to family dysfunction (Bumpass, Fagelman, & Brix, 1983; Fineman, 1980; Kazdin, 1990; Kolko & Kazdin, 1992). Saunders and Awad (1991) assert that adolescent firesetters are likely to experience parental separation, violence within the home, parental alcohol and drug abuse, or some form of physical or sexual abuse. Firesetters experience significantly more emotional neglect and physical abuse than other children of similar socioeconomic and geographic backgrounds (Thomas & Grimes, 1994). These juveniles also were more likely to have parents with limited parenting skills, limiting their chances to learn adequate coping skills (Swaffer & Hollin, 1995).

It also is interesting to note that low levels of sociability and social skills were identified for the parents of recidivist firesetters as well as the firesetters. Firesetters and their parents also were similar on measures of aggression, hostility, involvement in maladaptive behaviors, and difficult temperament (Kolko & Kazdin, 1991). Limitations that occur as a result of parents or families can affect the behaviors of juveniles. Absent mothers, fathers who abused drugs or alcohol, or mothers who abused alcohol or drugs were more likely to be found in the histories of firesetters than their respective controls (Showers & Pickrell, 1987). It is interesting to note that firesetting youth are more likely to come from families with parents who never married, though they were equally likely as control groups to come from families in which parents were divorced (Showers & Pickrell, 1987).

The impact of uninvolvement and limitations from parents and families on juvenile firesetters can be reduced with interventions. Increased fire-proofing within the home, improved psychosocial stability of individuals within the home, crisis intervention, and social service involvement have helped to redefine the roles of parents and firesetting youth. The importance of interindividual systems in impacting the behaviors of developing individuals cannot be overestimated (Bronfenbrenner, 1979; Stewart & Culver, 1982; Winget & Whitnam, 1973). It is thought that counseling and psychoeducational interventions can help a family to redefine the roles that lead to recidivism in firesetting youth (Jackson, Glass, & Hope, 1987; Kolko & Kazdin, 1992).

Economic stressors. Stressful environmental circumstances, individual crises, and limited support at home are often the precursors to property damage through use of fire. Low socioeconomic stability has been identified as a prime stressor that can affect the behaviors of juveniles (Schaenman, Hall, Schainblatt, Swartz, & Karter, 1977). Lower levels of income are correlated directly with an increased risk of residential fire. Schaenman et al. (1977) found that inter-city comparisons of fire rates were not as useful as census tracks that identified variables that are connected with socioeconomic status; such as (1) parental presence, or the percentage of children under the age of 18 years living with both parents; (2) poverty, defined as the percentage of persons whose incomes fell below the poverty line; and (3) under-education, or the percentage of persons over the age of 25 years who had fewer than eight years of schooling. In their study, 39 percent of the variance in fire rates could be connected with these three variables (Schaenman et al., 1977).

Socioeconomic variables that are related to higher incidents of firesetting in children also have been correlated to the level of stability found in the home (Federal Emergency Management Agency, 1995; Showers & Pickrell, 1987). Hanson, MacKay, Atkinson, & Staley (1995) strongly advise against fire professionals or managed care organizations limiting the opportunity for mental health involvement following the firesetting act. Limited access to counseling may increase the likelihood that firesetters will continue to engage in destructive behaviors (Hanson et al., 1995).

Environmental Distal Controls of Firesetting

School problems. At the present time, limited information exists about firesetters' experiences with school and its importance as a socializing agent. It was an interest of this study to examine the importance of school peers and teachers as they might influence the behaviors of firesetters.

Peer problems. Juvenile firesetters often are found to have difficulty interacting with others, including family, peers, and teachers (Showers & Pickrell, 1987). These limitations in juvenile ability to communicate thoughts and emotions are likely to reduce the opportunity for these youth to develop normative socialization skills (Kazdin, 1990). Such limited opportunities for communication and camaraderie may limit the psychosocial stability of these individuals, furthering their firesetting tendencies and other maladaptive behaviors (Heaven, 1994; Kazdin, 1990; Levin, 1976; Vandersall & Wiener, 1970).

Vandersall and Wiener (1970) assert that young firesetters rarely have significant friendships. Juvenile firesetters also have been identified as viewing themselves as loners, living outside their families or communities. Some firesetters indicate that they engage in firesetting to impress peers. Others have stated that they set fires because they did not have peers to play with, and engaging with fire as a way to pass the time (Blumberg, 1981; Fineman, 1995; Kolko & Kazdin, 1986b).

Youth firesetters differ in the ways that incendiaries are obtained or utilized, but many juveniles indicate that they receive incendiaries from peers. Moreover, juvenile firesetters differ in the peers they emulate (Kolko & Kazdin, 1986a). Vandersall and Wiener (1970) assert that many teenagers receive incendiaries from peers, which are later used to start fires. The presence of peers who smoke, peers that play with fire, peer pressure to participate in firesetting, or the presence of materials left around by parents or peers can all be factors which preclude the setting of a fire (Kolko & Kazdin, 1986a).

Firesetting may result from peer pressure or be initiated as a group activity, especially among adolescents. Adolescents also are more likely than younger children to involve peers in their firesetting and to brag about their destructive behaviors. As they attempt to gain status, adolescent firesetters often move onto larger and more destructive fires, gaining both confidence and experience (Showers & Pickrell, 1987; also see Eisler, 1972).

It also has been theorized that some young adults initiate firesetting as they attempt to accommodate adult roles and acquire a sense of control. Recidivism in adolescent firesetters has been associated with feelings of inability to control one's environment or aspects of one's life (locus of control) (Kolko & Kazdin, 1994; Kolko, Kazdin, & Meyer, 1985). Though firesetting in adolescents and young adults is often associated with maladaptive psychosocial patterns, by early adulthood, most firesetters are identified as being pathological or criminals (Levin, 1976; Schwartzman et al., 1994).

Firesetting Across Early Childhood and Adolescence

Examination of the differences between age groups also will improve professionals' understanding of this maladaptive behavior. Though a largely unexplored area of study, it is believed that maladaptive firesetting and the reasons for firesetting differ across early childhood and adolescence as a result of developmental changes (Jackson, Hope, & Glass, 1987; Kolko,

1985).

Patterson (1982) asserts that firesetters of different types and ages require different explanations for their firesetting. Previous studies have suggested that as children get older, their firesetting is directed away from their homes toward neighborhood buildings, dumpsters, automobiles, and schools (Schwartzman et al., 1994). It is hypothesized that juvenile firesetting follows an age-related developmental trend, with children (children ages 7 to 10) showing greater levels of firesetting than other age groups. Further, it is hypothesized that firesetting in young children is more likely to result in greater destructiveness to property and loss of life than the firesetting of any other age group.

Firesetting in Young Children (Ages 3 to 6 Years)

Studies of firesetting behavior in children are limited, even though it constitutes a fairly frequent and dangerous set of early childhood behaviors (Moore, Thompson-Pope, & Whited, 1996). In connection with an orientation to psychodynamic ideas, firesetting in young early childhood is often assumed to involve some inherent or biologically primary/instinctual drive (Levin, 1976). Firesetting in young children also is more likely to result in greater destructiveness to property and loss of life than the firesetting of any other age group (Showers & Pickrell, 1987).

However, firesetting in young children has been identified as being related to a neglectful family environment (Gaynor & Hatcher, 1987). Macht & Mack (1968) have asserted that the family environment of the early childhood firesetter is chaotic and limited in nurturing behaviors. Patterson (1982) believes that early childhood firesetters show the beginnings of antisocial behaviors. The externalization of emotions through maladaptive behaviors resembles adolescents who engage in similar violent acts. As a result of these theories, unwanted and unacceptable early childhood behaviors are thought to be largely the result of a neglectful and abusive home environment.

Kolko (1985) found that early childhood firesetters can be characterized as having multiple behavior problems with few internalizing behaviors, such as depression, but many externalizing behaviors, such as rule breaking, aggression, and destruction. Moreover, Vandersall and Wiener (1970) assert that young firesetters rarely have significant friendships, and have a tendency to view themselves as loners, living outside their families or communities. Hanson et al. (1995) strongly advise against limiting the opportunity for mental health involvement following the firesetting act. Limited access to counseling may increase the likelihood that the firesetter will continue to engage in destructive behaviors (Hanson et al., 1994).

Fire-safety skills. It is believed that toddlers and young children set fires out of a developmental need to explore their environments (Schwartzman et al., 1994). These young firesetters who accidentally set fires are likely to lack an understanding of the dangerousness of firesetting (Canter & Frizon, 1998; Lester, 1975). Many fire professionals believe that educating youth about fire safety and the dangers of firesetting can reduce the recidivism rate among juvenile firesetters (Federal Emergency Management Agency, 1996). Also, psychoeducational interventions may reduce recidivism rates in early childhood firesetters following the integration of fire safety measures within educational programming, general childcare systems, or family welfare schemes (Adler et al., 1994; Eisler, 1972).

Firesetting in Children (Ages 7 to 10 Years)

The primary source of information on firesetting behavior initiated by children is found within the Uniform Crime Report. The most recent Uniform Crime Report indicates that 11,000 juveniles were arrested for arson and firesetting in 1998. While juveniles below the age of 13 years were involved in 10% of all juvenile arrests, they were involved in a great proportion of arrests from property destruction and crimes of physical aggression, such as forcible rape (11%), nonviolent sexual offenses (18%), vandalism (19%), and arson (35%) (Williams, 1998). Firesetting behaviors are not typical behaviors for children or adolescents (Levin, 1976). Because many firesetters under the age of 12 years are diverted from the juvenile justice system, the real incidence of child firesetters is unknown (Federal Emergency Management Agency, 1996). Children between the ages of 7 and 12 years are the most understudied group of all firesetters (Kolko, 1985).

Early learning experiences. Exposure to fire at an early age may increase the likelihood that children will engage in maladaptive firesetting behaviors (Jackson, Glass, & Hope, 1987; Kolko & Kazdin, 1986, 1991; Yarnell, 1940). Parents and other significant family members serve as models that can either reinforce or reject their children's firesetting behavior. Learning experiences and cues that can preclude maladaptive firesetting include early modeling of inappropriate use of fire, early interest and direct experience with fire, and availability of adult models and incendiary materials.

Firesetting in Early Adolescents (Ages 11 to 14 Years)

Firesetting in this age group has been found to differ for motivational reasons as well. Showers and Pickrell (1987) found that those over the age of 12 are motivated to use fire for revenge. Achenbach (1966) theorized that internalization or externalization of behaviors largely impacts aggression in children and early adolescents. Early adolescents who internalize emotions tend to report depressive or somatic symptoms, while juveniles who externalize emotions through their behaviors show a higher level of acting out against others. Achenbach placed maladaptive firesetting behaviors within this category. Kolko and Kazdin (1991) have supported these findings, reporting higher levels of antisocial behaviors, higher levels of behavioral problems, and higher levels of hostility and aggression in early adolescent firesetters. Examination of this age group shows that most adolescent firesetters are at the lower end of the age group, around 13-14 years of age (Schwartzman et al., 1994).

Many youthful firesetters are attracted to and "invested in" fire (Macht & Mack, 1968). Few studies have been performed which have examined the motivation behind firesetting behaviors. However, it has been largely hypothesized that firesetting behaviors may be caused by such motives as revenge, jealousy, spite, or anger (Fineman, 1980; Kolko & Kazdin, 1986a; Yarnell, 1940).

Firesetting in Late Adolescents (Ages 15 to 18 Years)

Firesetting among late adolescents typically involves delinquent activities, and usually occurs as a result of peer pressure or group oriented activities. Attention-seeking behaviors are often a factor involved in their firesetting, as is the desire to get a reaction from parents, authorities and emergency services (Schwartzman et al., 1994). Research indicates that a subgroup of antisocial recidivist firesetters exists among young offenders (Hanson et al., 1994). Late adolescents who set fires often start with small and insignificant fires, then move onto larger and more destructive fires as they gain confidence and experience. Teenagers also are more likely than younger children to involve peers in their firesetting and to brag about their destructive behaviors.

Macht and Mack (1968) found that fathers of adolescent firesetters were frequently involved in some way with fire in their occupations (e.g. – fireman, furnace stoker), and that their children had been fascinated with their professions at an early age. Similar results were found by Yarnell (1940). Exposure to fire at an earlier age may correlate with early firesetting, which has been identified as leading to larger and more destructive firesetting behaviors across time (Grolnick, Cole, Laurentis, & Schwartzman, 1990; Schwartzman et al., 1994; Yarnell, 1940).

Hanson et al. (1995) studied 25 male delinquents (mean age 13.8 years) who had been legally charged for setting fires. They were compared to a group of age and sex-matched delinquents who had legal charges filed against them that were not related to firesetting. Groups were compared on demographic variables, on measures of delinquency, and on fire-related histories. The only significant difference to emerge was a higher proportion of past firesetting in the group with fire-related charges (see Grolnick et al., 1990; Kolko & Kazdin, 1994).

The current study is based on the premise that aberrant behavior, such as firesetting, occurs because some children and adolescents suffer from weak or nonexistent bonds to society, which causes them to behave in socially unacceptable ways. Juvenile firesetting may be one example of larger problems with aggression, deviance, or difficulty externalizing behaviors.

Typology of Juvenile Firesetters

Patterson (1982) asserts that firesetters of different types and ages require different explanations for their firesetting behaviors. Professionals also may find it helpful to identify the type of firesetter with which they are working. Though some in the field have differentiated between firesetters based on severe versus nonsevere groupings (Sakheim & Osborn, 1999), other classification systems have been suggested as being more helpful to fire professionals and mental health workers. Jones, Ribbe, & Cunningham (1994) suggest that systems of classification should parallel the motivations that spur juvenile firesetters to play with fire. Fineman (1995) offers seven commonly identified types.

Curiosity Firesetter

Curious firesetters are typically young children (juveniles ages 3 to 6 years) who engage in firesetting as experimentation. When asked why they started a fire, curiosity firesetters tend to respond that they did so in a desire to watch a flame. In some instances, hyperactivity or attention deficit disorder may be present. Curiosity firesetters hold no intent to cause harm. Curiosity firesetting is the traditional early childhood diagnosis for most firesetting children ages seven years and below.

Curiosity firesetters often show remorse for their behaviors following the incident (Kolko & Kazdin, 1991), and tend not to understand the consequences of their behaviors. It is thought that most children are inherently curious about fire. However, curiosity firesetters are likely to have early involvement with firesetting, and are generally more interested in fire than other types of juvenile firesetters (Kolko & Kazdin, 1991).

Accidental Firesetter

Accidental firesetters are usually children under the age of 11 years. However, this category of firesetters also may include teenagers engaging in experimental firesetting or those that are playing scientist. Young adult accidents or adult carelessness may fall into this group. Accidental firesetters do not intend to cause harm. For the most part, accidental firesetting is not the result of neglectful or abusive home environments (Canter & Frizon, 1998; Federal Emergency Management Agency, 1996).

The "Cry for Help" Firesetter

The cry for help firesetter often co-occurs with the diagnoses of attention deficit hyperactivity disorder, depression not otherwise specified, major depression, oppositional defiant disorder, or post traumatic stress disorder. These children and adolescents may engage in maladaptive firesetting behaviors in an attempt to bring attention to their parental or familial dysfunction (Fineman, 1995). This group traditionally is defined by offenders who consciously or subconsciously wish to bring attention to intrapersonal dysfunction (depression), or to interpersonal dysfunction (abuse at home, presence during parental conflict). Although these firesetters are generally not thought to cause harm or damage (Federal Emergency Management Agency, 1996), their inability to appropriately express themselves can cause serious personal or property injury. "Cry for help" firesetters generally have a acceptable prognosis for treatment (Fineman, 1995).

A subgroup of "cry for help" firesetters are those individuals who set fires in order to be seen as would be hero types - seeking the attention of peers or the community in order to discover or help put out fires they start. The "cry for help firesetter" is the traditional diagnosis for abused children.

Delinquent Firesetter

Delinquent firesetting is theorized to have a developmental trend. Delinquent tendencies are thought to begin during preadolescence and increase throughout adolescence. The delinquent type includes those that set fire for profit and those that set fire to cover another crime. This group tends to engage in vandalism and hate crimes. During preadolescence delinquent firesetters show some empathy for others (Harris & Rice, 1996). However, adolescent delinquent firesetters show little empathy for others, or little conscience for their behaviors. Though they have limited empathy for other members of their families/communities, adolescent delinquent types rarely harm others with fire. Significant property damage is common. As young adults, delinquent firesetters may attempt to harm others.

Kolko & Kazdin (1991) found that higher rates of other deviant behaviors immediately preceded firesetting recidivism when compared with other juveniles that had been psychiatric inpatients. As a group they show the greatest amount of deviancy and behavioral dysfunction. Firesetting behavior in this group is extinguished more easily than the other personality and behavior problems that accompany the firesetting (Showers & Pickrell, 1987).

Severely Disturbed Firesetter

Those few youth firesetters who have been diagnosed as severely disturbed firesetters are diagnosed by a wide variety of individual pathologies, such as post-traumatic stress disorder, general anxiety disorder, conduct disorder, and oppositional defiant disorder (Jones, Ribbe, & Cunningham, 1994; Lowenstein, 1989). Moore, Thompson-Pope, Whited (1996) found that firesetters, when compared with other inpatient adolescent boys without a history of firesetting, scored significantly higher on three clinical scales: mania, schizophrenia, and psychastenia.

Unlike the "cry for help" firesetter who tend to show similar symptomatology as a result of environmental circumstances, these children are likely to have early signs as a result of individual psychopathology. Severely disturbed children are more likely than other types of

Table One

Typology of Firesetters

Type of Firesetter	Characteristics
1. Curiosity Type	Younger children who do not understand consequences of their behavior. Desire is to watch the flame. Hyperactivity or attention deficit may be present. No intent to cause harm. Traditional early childhood diagnosis.
2. Accidental Type	Usually involves children under 11 years of age. Teenagers playing scientist. The fire results from no destructive motive to create fire.
3. The "Cry for Help" Type	Includes those offenders who consciously or subconsciously wish to bring attention to an interpersonal dysfunction (depression) to an interpersonal dysfunction (abuse at home, vicarious observation of parental conflict). Not meant to harm people. Acceptable prognosis for treatment. Firefighter who sets fires or adult/juvenile "would be hero types" - seeking the attention of peers or the community in order to discover or help put out fires they start. Traditional early childhood diagnosis for abused children.
4. Delinquent Type	Includes the fire for profit type and the cover another crime type. Interest in vandalism and hate crimes is noteworthy. As juveniles, this type shows little empathy for others. Shows little conscious. Juvenile types rarely harm others with fire. Significant property damage is common. As adults, significant percentage harm others. Firesetting behavior is more easily extinguished than other personality and behavior problems that usually accompany the firesetting.
5. Severely Disturbed Type	Includes those juveniles who seek to harm themselves, paranoid, and psychotic types, for which the fixation of fire may be a major factor in the development of a mental disorder. Sensory aspects of the fire are sufficiently reinforcing to cause fires to be frequently set. Pyromaniac is a sub-type - sensory reinforcement is often powerful enough for significant harm to occur. Prognosis is guarded with this group.
6. Cognitively Impaired Type	Includes the retarded and the organically impaired types. Tends to avoid intention harm, lack acceptable judgment. Significant property damage is common. Prognostically, they are acceptable therapy candidates. Also included in this group are persons with severe learning disabilities, those affected by fetal alcohol syndrome, or by drugs taken by their mother during pregnancy.
7. Sociocultural Type	Includes the uncontrolled mass hysteria type, the attention to cause type, the religious type, and the satanic type. Arsonists who set fires primarily for the support they get for doing so by groups within their communities. Those who may set fires in the midst of civil unrest, and are either enraged and enticed by the activity of others and follow suit, or set fires with deliberation in order to call attention to the righteousness of their cause. Frequently lose control and harm others. Most are amenable to treatment.

Note. From "A Model for the Qualitative Analysis of Child and Adult Fire Deviant Behavior," by K. Fineman, 1995, American Journal of Forensic Psychology, 13, p. 34. Adapted with permission of the author.

firesetters to be found in an inpatient population, and also showed higher incidents of recidivism than outpatient populations (Kolko & Kazdin, 1988). However, such diagnoses have not been found to adequately characterize the conditions that surround these children and adolescents (Jones et al., 1994; Rice & Harris, 1996; Showers & Pickrell, 1987).

Also included in this category are paranoid and psychotic types, for whom the fixation of fire may be a major factor in the development of a mental disorder. The pyromaniac is a sub-type of the severely disturbed category. Prognosis is guarded with this group. Though social neglect and parental dysfunction are likely to be correlated with firesetters identified as severely disturbed, further research needs to be initiated which answers the question of how parental dysfunction and social neglect contribute to firesetting behavior rather than other disturbing behaviors exhibited by the firesetter (Heath et al., 1976).

Cognitively Impaired Firesetter

Cognitively impaired firesetters typically include those children or adolescents who hold diagnoses, such as attention deficit disorder, attention deficit hyperactivity disorder, learning disabilities, or who are mildly mentally retarded, as well as those youth who are retarded or have some organic brain dysfunction. Also included in this group are persons with severe learning disabilities, those affected by fetal alcohol syndrome, or by drugs taken by their mother during pregnancy.

The view that most young firesetters are of low intelligence has been largely discounted in recent years by Showers and Pickrell (1987) who reported that disobedience and aggression, as well as emotional and physical abuse are better predictors of firesetting behaviors. Lower intelligence in juvenile firesetters may be better explained as a result of growing up under economic disadvantage and limited educational opportunities. Those firesetters who are cognitively impaired tend to avoid intentional harm, but lack acceptable judgment about matchplay and control of fire. Significant property damage is common with this group. Prognostically, they are acceptable candidates for therapy and educational interventions.

In a study of mentally challenged arsonists, Barnett et al. (1997) found that mentally-challenged firesetters, when compared with other types of firesetters did not have a history of deviancy, legal offenses, or other forms of law breaking related to vandalism. However, the researchers did find that mentally challenged firesetters had a higher rate of recidivism than non-mentally-challenged firesetters (Barnett et al., 1997). It also has been suggested that individuals with a learning disability who set fires do so for the excitement of the destructiveness or the control they receive from fire play (Murphy & Claire, 1996).

Sociocultural Firesetter

More often than not, these firesetters are young adult or adult arsonists who set fires primarily for the support they get for doing so by groups within their communities. Those sociocultural types who set fires typically are in the midst of civil unrest, and either are enraged or enticed by the activity of others and follow suit, or set fires with deliberation in order to call attention to the righteousness of their cause. These firesetters frequently lose control and harm others.

Levin (1976) suggests that an analysis of firesetting behaviors needs to include whether the firesetter acted as an individual or within a group. He also suggests that the sociocultural type is most likely to utilize fire in order to embarrass or intimidate an opponent when involving a group of firesetters, but that individual firesetting is more likely to be about arson-for-profit.

Summary

An examination of the literature to date on firesetters shows that a variety of different characteristics can define specific types of firesetters. Furthermore, firesetting behaviors appear to differ as a result of both individual and environmental circumstances. An appropriate review of firesetting should include an examination of the firesetter's history; such as with prior fire learning experiences, cognitive and behavioral reviews, and parent and family influences and stressors.

CHAPTER THREE
METHODOLOGY

Introduction

Data used in the present study were drawn from the Marion County Arson Investigation Network (MCAIN). All data and methods of data gathering conform to Federal Emergency Management Agency (FEMA) standards. The data set required adaptation and cleaning to be subject to analysis for this study. Thus, the following chapter will 1) describe the MCAIN data gathering protocol, 2) define the structure of the data set, 3) define the procedures for creating the data file, and 4) discuss the participants of the study.

Data Gathering Protocol

The complete data gathering protocol included data collection at four data points: (a) the firesetting events, (b) the fire site evaluation of the event and the fire site interview by professionals, (c) a referral by fire professionals to the Fire Stop psychoeducational program with MCAIN, and (d) the Fire Stop program interview. The Fire Stop program interview included an interview of family members using the Family Fire Risk Interview Form (Fineman, 1997a), the Juvenile Fire Risk Interview Form (Fineman, 1997b), and the Parent Fire Risk Questionnaire (Fineman, 1997c).

Firesetting Events

Firesetting events were operationalized as any occurrence of fire in which a juvenile was identified as the instigator of a fire. The set fire could have been intentional or unintentional, and the effects of the fire could range from minor to substantial. Fire professionals were contacted about firesetting events by several referral sources, including parents, neighbors, school personnel, and mental health professionals. Fire professionals visited the fire event site within 90 minutes of the referral. Fires that were investigated by MCAIN have originated at a variety of sites; including homes, schools, abandoned buildings, abandoned cars, alleyways, and trash dumpsters.

Fire Site Evaluation of Event

Initial information regarding a firesetting event was obtained at the fire locale by way of a site survey. An initial fire site interview was performed at the locale where the fire occurred. Fire professionals called to the scene of the fire were responsible for completing a narrative record at the time of the investigation. Fire professionals included either arson investigators or police officers with the juvenile justice system. Fire professionals were certified to perform arson investigations following training with the Indiana State Fire Marshal's Office and/or the United States Fire Administration.

Fire professionals were responsible for completing a standard arson investigation form designed by the Federal Emergency Management Agency (FEMA, 1988). Information regarding the youth's firesetting was taken from interviews performed at the site of the fire. Investigators collected statements from the juvenile firesetter(s), their family members, and other witnesses of the fire. Investigators also completed an estimated dollar amount of property loss resulting from the juvenile's firesetting.

Referral to Fire Stop Program

Following the arson investigation, the fire professional referred the juvenile to the Fire Stop program with MCAIN. Referrals were made to the Fire Stop program if the firesetter was between the ages of 3 years and 18 years old at the time of the event. Juveniles and their parents scheduled appointments with the director of MCAIN's Fire Stop program within 10 days of the firesetting event.

Juvenile firesetters were to have been referred to the Fire Stop program by fire professionals following the fire site interviews. However, firesetters also could have been referred to the Fire Stop program by other professionals, such as teachers, school counselors, physicians, counselors, social workers, or state caseworkers. If referral was performed by a professional other than a fire professional, the standard arson investigation form was completed by the Fire Stop program staff. Data points collected during the referral were general demographic information about the firesetter and their family. Demographic variables were added to the information obtained during the fire site evaluation.

Fire Stop Program staff. The Marion County Arson Investigation Network Fire Stop Program is headed by a fire professional with over 30 years experience, who was the first professional in Indiana to initiate a state-run psychoeducation program for firesetters in 1984. Prior to her work with psychoeducation, she was an arson investigator for Wayne Township Fire Department for 21 years. She has served as a facilitator for the United States Fire Administration certification committee for arson investigation education, and is a member of the Indiana State Fire Marshal's Office Juvenile Firesetter Committee.

Fire Stop Program curriculum. The MCAIN Fire Stop Program includes secondary investigation of the firesetting event, as well as a 3-hour psychoeducational intervention program for juvenile firesetters and their families. In addition to completion of a fire risk evaluation (see Fineman, 1997a, 1997b, 1997c), the Fire Stop program provides incident-specific and age-appropriate education for firesetters and their family. Data used in the present study included information taken during the secondary investigation of the firesetting event as well as the psychoeducational intervention program. Data points included information completed on the Federal Emergency Management Agency Fire Risk Evaluation forms (1997a, 1997b, 1997c), as well as a separate narrative record provided by the Fire Stop director.

Fire Stop Program Interview

After arriving for their scheduled interview at the Marion County Arson Investigation Unit Headquarters, parents and children entered an office that included a large table surrounded by chairs. The office included pictures on surrounding walls espousing information on fire prevention. The table was cleared, except for the juvenile's data record and blank interview forms. A videorecorder was stationed in the corner, which would later be used for the psychoeducational portion of the program.

Data collection took place during a scheduled three-hour interview between the fire professional, the firesetter, and the firesetter's parent/guardian following referral to the MCAIN Fire Stop program. In most instances juvenile firesetters were accompanied mostly by their biological mothers. Few interviews were identified that included both parents and few interviews were identified where children were brought in by male guardians or fathers. Interview protocol follows the recommended interview format designed by the Federal Emergency Management Agency (FEMA, 1988). Parents and participants were told that they were to engage in a brief discussion regarding their firesetting behaviors. Participants and their parents completed questionnaires and interview questions as fulfillment of mandatory program requirements.

Following referral to the program, a MCAIN data record was created for the juvenile firesetter. Each data record of the MCAIN database includes demographic information, the nature of the firesetter's behaviors, the firesetting incident, and whether or not the individual followed-up with any counseling following the fire. Four primary pieces of information are included in each data record: (a) narrative information taken from the fire site interview, (b) the Family Fire Risk Interview Form (Fineman, 1997a), (c) the Juvenile Fire Risk Interview Form (Fineman, 1997b), and (d) the Parent Fire Risk Questionnaire (Fineman, 1997c). Psychometric data for each of these forms are provided in Chapter Four of this document.

Family Fire Risk Interview Form. First, parents and juveniles completed the Family Fire Risk Interview Form (Fineman, 1997a, see Appendix A). The director of the Fire Stop Program was responsible for reading questions from the interview form in a semi-structured format. The director indicated that most questions during this time are answered by the parent/guardian, but juveniles are able to interject their ideas and beliefs during the interview (Spurlin, 1999, personal communication). Completion time for this 65-question interview form was approximately 30 minutes.

The Family Fire Risk Interview Form includes two scales, a Parent Scale and a Child Scale. Parent responses made on the parent scale relate to statements regarding the parents, while responses made on the child scale relate to statements regarding the child. The questionnaire includes 65 questions in Likert Scale format. Each scale ranges from 1 (Rarely to never) to 3 (Frequently). Parents were required to answer statements such as [my child has] "learning problems at school," [my child is] "physically violent," and [my child has] "curiosity about fire." High scores on the Family Fire Risk Interview Form reflect greater psychosocial risk of recidivism.

Juvenile Fire Risk Interview Form. Following completion of the Family Fire Risk Interview Form, the parent and juvenile are separated so that the juvenile could complete a second interview form. After the parent had left the room, the juvenile completed the Juvenile Fire Risk Interview Form (Fineman, 1997b, see Appendix B). The director of the Fire Stop Program was responsible for reading questions from the interview form in a semi-structured format. Completion time for this interview form was approximately 45 minutes.

The inventory includes 65 questions, some forced choice format questions and some questions in Likert Scale format. The Likert Scale questions used a scale ranging from 1 (Rarely to never) to 3 (Frequently). Juveniles were required to answer statements such as "Have you gotten in trouble at school?," "Do you think your friends are a bad influence on you?," and "Do you usually do things you are asked to do?." High scores on the Juvenile Fire Risk Interview Form reflect greater psychosocial risk of recidivism.

Parent Fire Risk Questionnaire. Following completion of the Family Fire Risk Interview Form, parents were asked to leave the room to complete the Parent Fire Risk Questionnaire (Fineman, 1997c; see Appendix C). Parents were provided assistance if they had difficulty understanding questions or reading the material provided to them. The questionnaires were filled out in a room adjacent to where their child was being interviewed. The questionnaire required approximately 20 minutes to complete.

The questionnaire includes 116 questions in Likert Scale format. Using a scale ranging from 1 (Rarely to never) to 3 (Frequently), parents were required to answer statements such as [my child has] "learning problems at school," [my child is] "physically violent," and [my child has] "curiosity about fire." High scores on the Parent Fire Risk Questionnaire reflect greater psychosocial risk of recidivism.

After completing the questionnaire, the parent and firesetters reunited and finished the interview section of the Fire Stop program by reviewing the information obtained. The information obtained during the interview is used to identify the likelihood of recidivist firesetting behaviors. Following completion of all interview materials, the Fire Stop facilitator tallies the responses on all three instruments, organizing a disposition of the case. If the preponderance (over 80%) of the critical responses is in the low to moderate risk level, an educational intervention would be appropriate. If the majority of the responses are in the high risk level, a referral to a mental health professional is required (FEMA, 1988).

Status of MCAIN Data Files

Each data record included a fire event narrative, a referral, the Fire Stop Interview narrative, and the FEMA instruments. In the event that a firesetter engages in recidivist behaviors, all information was included for each individual fire event. First, the MCAIN records for juvenile firesetters were accessed. MCAIN records are organized by month and year, and included juvenile firesetters from January 1994 to December 1999. For the purposes of this study, information was taken from juvenile firesetting records obtained from January 1994 through December 1999 (Fineman, 1997a, 1997b, 1997c).

The records are housed in manila folders on site at MCAIN headquarters. Each manila folder contains demographic information, completed FEMA (Fineman, 1997a, 1997b, 1997c) forms, a narrative record from the preliminary on-site interviews taken at the time of the fire, and any correspondence between MCAIN staff and juvenile justice regarding the incident. Supplemental materials, such as juvenile court records on the individual and narrative notes made by the director also were included in a data record (Spurlin, personal communication, 1999). Prior to recording data to the research data file, all identifying labels were expunged.

Creating a Data File

An electronic dataset separate from the MCAIN datafile was created using the MCAIN records. Information was organized from the MCAIN files into a separate database using the SPSS data management system. No information was transferred directly from MCAIN computer files to the current study's computerized SPSS data file. In other words all data utilized in the present study were organized and entered by the researcher for the sole purpose of this investigation.

Decisions regarding the data. Only data records that include the FEMA (Fineman, 1997a, 1997b, 1997c) forms and the narrative record from the preliminary on-site interviews taken at the time of the fire were utilized. 91% of cases were included of all juveniles who were referred to the Fire Stop program. Files completed prior to the introduction of the revised FEMA (Fineman, 1997a, 1997b, 1997c) instruments were included in analysis for this study. Though the instruments were revised in 1997, revisions were cosmetic in nature, and the wording of questions and organization of the questionnaires has remained the same since 1994.

Criteria for exclusion included blank FEMA (Fineman, 1997a, 1997b, 1997c) forms, an absence of the narrative record from the preliminary on-site interview, or a failure on the part of the MCAIN staff or parent/guardian to complete the necessary FEMA instruments. In the event that a file was missing a narrative record from the preliminary on-site interview, attempts were made to access police records that are likely to contain this narrative.

Missing data. Missing data were likely to result from questions that were neglected during the completion of the FEMA forms. The missing responses would differentially jeopardize the reliability of that record. In the event that an entire scale is missing from an inventory, the individual record was excluded from data analysis. In the event that individual questions were not completed on a inventory, but that a majority of the scale was completed, the median item value was substituted for the data point.

Miscoded data. Miscoded data included any computer data that does not match hard data taken from the MCAIN records, as well as any subscale score that is beyond the appropriate range for that scale. In the event that miscoded data were identified, it was recoded using information taken from the MCAIN file records. In the event that miscoded data could not be taken from the MCAIN records, values were identified by computer records held at the Marion County courthouse. Finally, when information could not be obtained by performing the previous methods, median values for those questions were used in the place of the miscoded data.

Measures

Demographic Factors

Demographic information was obtained from the Family Fire Risk Interview Form (Fineman, 1997a) completed by the parent/guardian at the time of Fire Stop Program interview. Information obtained included child's age, race, sex, level of education, school enrollment, number of siblings, parent's level of education, and parent's present job.

Age groups. Four age groups of firesetters were identified. Early childhood firesetters were defined as being between the ages of 3 to 6 years of age ($n = 255$). Child firesetters were defined as being between the ages of 7 to 10 years of age ($n = 312$). Early adolescent firesetters were defined as being between the ages of 11 to 14 years of age ($n = 117$). Late adolescent firesetters were defined as being between the ages of 15 to 18 years of age ($n = 204$).

Gender. Gender was classified as being either male ($n = 663$) or female ($n = 225$).

Family configuration. Family configuration and caregiver status were identified from information taken from the Family Fire Risk Interview Form (Fineman, 1997a). Status of the caregiver was divided between adoptive caregivers or biological caregivers. Caregivers were classified as either being males ($n = 1$) or females ($n = 57$). Parents were similarly classified as either fathers ($n = 7$) or mothers ($n = 823$). Family configuration for both parents was defined as being one of six classifications: single ($n = 112$), married ($n = 161$), divorced ($n = 78$), widowed ($n = 10$), separated ($n = 321$), or remarried ($n = 206$). When referring to their marital status, the caregiver/parent was asked to refer to their present status. Separate information also was taken of all individuals living in the home, including ages and relationships to the firesetter. Information on the living arrangements of the firesetter also was obtained (such as child living with grandparents, but away from mother and father, etc.).

Race. Race of participants and their parents was identified from information taken from the Family Fire Risk Interview Form (Fineman, 1997a). Race was characterized by the caregiver/parent's response, and included such categories as Caucasian ($n = 501$), African-American ($n = 334$), Hispanic American ($n = 17$), Asian American ($n = 2$), Black Hispanic ($n = 0$), Native American ($n = 0$), or Biracial ($n = 17$).

Socioeconomic status. A limitation of the present study was the lack of information pertaining to socioeconomic status. Failure to include such information was the lack of items on the FEMA (Fineman, 1997a, 1997b, 1997c) forms.

School. Information on the child's school was identified from information taken from the Family Fire Risk Interview Form (Fineman, 1997a). Information included the name of the school, the school address, and the student's grade.

Predictor Variables

Predictor variables included individual and environmental characteristics taken from data obtained during the fire site interview and Fire Stop Program interview. Individual characteristics included an affinity for aggression, and affinity for delinquency, and externalization of emotions. Environmental characteristics included proximal controls (family problems) and distal controls (school problems and peer problems).

Individual Characteristics

An affinity for aggression. An affinity for aggression was defined through a set of items referring to homicidal thoughts and plans, being the subject of or witness to domestic violence, engaging in cruelty to smaller children or animals, and engaging in physical aggression towards others (including parents and teachers). Perceptions of firesetters' level of aggression were addressed using information taken from the Parent Fire Risk Questionnaire (Fineman, 1997c). Each form included statements on information relating to aggression with responses ranging from 1 (low aggression) to 3 (high aggression). Respondents were given statements such as "Fights with siblings," and "Excessive and uncontrolled anger" This scale included 14 statements (see Table 2). Internal consistency for the scale was fair, with a Cronbach's alpha of .67.

Table 2

Questions identified for Affinity for Aggression scale

Physically fights with peers
Excessive and uncontrolled verbal anger
Physically violent
Cruel to Animals
Cruel to Children
Expresses anger by damaging the property of others
Destroys own toys (ages 3-6)
Destroys own toys (ages 7-18)
Severe behavior difficulties
Expresses anger by hurting others
Temper tantrums
Fighting with siblings
Expresses anger by hurting self or something he likes
Destroys toys/property of others

An affinity for delinquency. An affinity for delinquency was defined through a set of items that identified behaviors that were bothersome to caregivers (e.g., highly stubborn behavior, lying, truancy, running away from home) or that inflict harm or property loss on other (vandalism, theft, violent acts). Parents' perceptions of the firesetters' delinquency was addressed using information taken from the Parent Fire Risk Questionnaire (Fineman, 1997c). Participants and their families were asked for information relating to delinquency with responses ranging from 1 (low delinquency) to 3 (high delinquency). Respondents and their families were given such statements as "Behavior problems at school," and "Truant/school runaway." This scale included 16 questions and statements (see Table 3). Internal consistency for the scale was acceptable, with an identified Cronbach's alpha of .90.

Table 3

Questions identified on Affinity for Delinquency scale

Behavior problems at school
Truant/school runaway
Shows off for peers
Steals
Is/was in a gang
Disobeys
Has been in trouble with the police
Lies
Uses drugs or alcohol
Jealous of peers/siblings
Unacceptable showing off
Sexual activity with others
Set occupied structure on fire
Runs away from home
In trouble at home
Was/is in a cult

Externalization of emotions. Externalization of emotions was defined by items indicating any malicious mischief, covering of a crime, or voluntary act that was committed to express negative affect or express emotions inappropriately. Perceptions of firesetters' externalization of emotions were addressed using information taken from the Parent Fire Risk Questionnaire (Fineman, 1997c). Each form included statements relating to externalization of emotions with responses ranging from 1 (low externalization) to 3 (high externalization). Respondents and their families were given such statements as "Lack of concentration," and "Depressed mood or withdrawn." This scale included 27 statements (see Table 4). Internal consistency for the scale was fair, with a Cronbach's alpha of .79.

Environmental Characteristics

Proximal Controls

Family problems. Family problems were defined through a set of items that referred to the impact and pressures that the family may unknowingly place on firesetters to engage in firesetting as a result of parent/family dysfunction or limited opportunity for normative life experiences. Perceptions of firesetters' family problems were addressed using information taken from the Parent Fire Risk Questionnaire (Fineman, 1997c). Each statement included information relating to family problems with responses ranging from 1 (low family problems) to 3 (high family problems). Respondents and their families were asked such statements as, "Extensive absences by father/mother," and "Marriage is unhappy." This scale included 14 statements (see Table 5). Internal consistency for the scale was identified as a Cronbach's alpha value of .61.

Table 4

Questions identified on Externalization of Emotions scale

Lack of concentration
Impulsive (acts before he/she thinks)
Impatient
Shyness
Stomach aches
Nightmares
Sleeps too deep or problem waking up
Anxiety (nervousness)
Has twitches
Cries
Bites Nails
Vomits
Aches and pains
Extreme mood swings
Depressed mood or withdrawal
Constipation
Diarrhea

Table 4

Questions identified on Externalization of Emotions scale

Sleep walking
Phobias
General Fears
Strange thought patterns
Bizarre/illogical/irrational speech
Out of touch with reality
Strange quality about child
Destroys own property
Severe depression or withdrawal
Poor or no eye contact

Table 5

Questions identified on Family problems scale

Need for excessive security
Need for affection
Others in family set fires (past or present)
Excessive absences by father
Excessive absences by mother
Family has moved
Has seen a counselor/therapist
Other family member has seen a counselor/therapist
Makes attempts at age appropriate independence from parents
Parent or sibling with serious health problem
Marriage is unhappy
Mother's /female caregiver discipline is effective
Father's/male caregiver discipline is effective
Conflicts in family

Distal Controls

School problems. It was an interest of this study to identify whether the school environment and its participants would have an influence on firesetters' desires to engage in firesetting. Perceptions of the firesetters' family problems were addressed using information taken from the Parent Fire Risk Questionnaire (Fineman, 1997c). Parents' perceptions of the firesetters' school behaviors and relationships were defined through a set of items referring to information relating to school problems with responses ranging from 1 (low school problems) to 3 (high school problems). Respondents and their families were asked such statements as "Hyperactivity at school," and "Listens to teacher(s)/school authorities." This scale included 6 statements (see Table 6). Internal consistency for the scale was fair, with a Cronbach's alpha was .70.

Table 6

Questions identified on School problems scale

Hyperactivity at school
Learning problems at school
Fantasizes (day dreaming)
Likes school
Listens to teacher(s)/school authorities
Shows age appropriate interest in future school/jobs/career

Peer problems. Peer problems were defined through a set of items that referred to the impact and pressures of peers on firesetters to engage in firesetting, as well as the firesetters' failure to be involved in normative peer relationships. Perceptions of the firesetters' peer problems were addressed using information taken from the Parent Fire Risk Questionnaire (Fineman, 1997c). Each statement included information relating to peers with responses ranging from 1 (low peer problems) to 3 (high peer problems). Respondents and their parents were asked such statements as, "Relationships are socially appropriate," and "Plays with other kids." This scale included 12 questions and statements, with a Cronbach's alpha of .77 (see Table 7).

Table 7

Questions identified on Peer Problems scale

Tries to please everyone
Relationships are socially appropriate
Withdraws from peers/group
Is a poor loser
Easily led by peers
Plays with other children
Shows appropriate peer affection
Plays alone (not even with adults)
Picked on by peers
Has many friends
Participates in sports
Is a loner

Other Independent Variables Examined

Enuresis

The presence of enuresis was identified using information taken from the Parent Fire Risk Questionnaire (Fineman, 1997c). Juveniles were either identified as having problems with enuresis or not.

Cruelty to Animals

The presence of cruelty to animals was identified using information taken from the Parent Fire Risk Questionnaire (Fineman, 1997c). Juveniles were either identified as having problems with cruel behavior toward animals or not.

Dependent Variables

Types of Firesetters

Jones, Ribbe, & Cunningham (1994) suggest that systems of classification should parallel the motivations that spur juvenile firesetters to play with fire. Fineman (1995) offers seven commonly identified types which were used in the present study: curiosity firesetters, accidental firesetters, cry for help firesetters, delinquent firesetters, severely disturbed firesetters, cognitively impaired firesetters, and sociocultural firesetters. Identification of firesetters was taken from the Fire Stop Program Interview.

Recidivism

The presence of recidivistic behaviors was identified using information taken from the Juvenile Fire Risk Questionnaire (Fineman, 1997b). Juveniles were either identified as having problems with recidivism or not.

Magnitude of Fire Damage

The magnitude of fire damage was identified using information taken from the fire site evaluation of the fire event. The magnitude of fire damage was an estimate based on the dollar amount that resulted from damage caused by the fire. Due to the variable nature of fire, the magnitude of fire damage was an extremely unstable variable, and ranged from no damage to several thousands of dollars.

Participants

Records from 255 early child firesetters (ages 3 to 6 years), 312 child firesetters (ages 7 to 10 years), 117 early adolescent firesetters (ages 11 to 14 years), and 204 late adolescent firesetters (ages 15 to 18 years) who were referred to Marian County Arson Investigation Network (MCAIN) for firesetting behaviors were analyzed. As a result of many firesetters over the age of 12 being referred for incarceration rather than psychoeducation, the sampling of juveniles at or above this age is believed to be limited. For the purposes of the study, the entire MCAIN database was used. Firesetters in the MCAIN data file range in age from 3 to 19 years old. There was a greater preponderance of late adolescent firesetters than the other considered groups (see Kolko, 1985 for a review). There also were a higher number of male firesetters than female firesetters (see Table 8).

Table 8

Review of Sample with Gender x Age Group

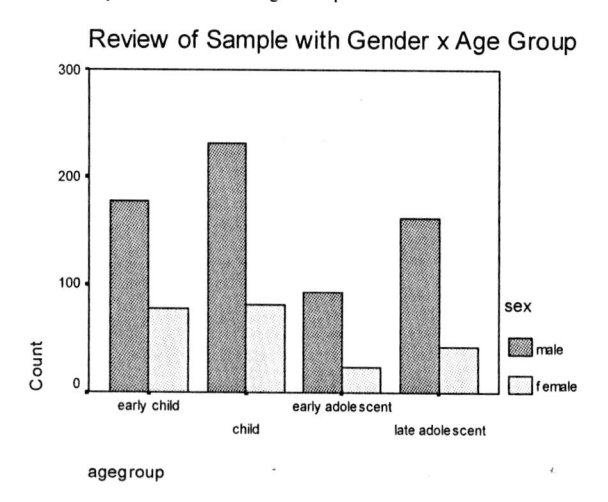

Table 9

Means, Standard Deviations, and Level of Skew for Variables

Variable	N	Minimum	Maximum	Mean	Std. Deviation	Skewness	
	Statistic	Statistic	Statistic	Statistic	Statistic	Statistic	Std. Error
Age	888	12.00	249.00	106.902	46.4303	.288	.082
Aggression	888	14.00	39.00	21.8750	7.1602	.958	.082
Cruelty to Animals	888	1.00	2.00	1.1824	.3864	1.647	.082
Delinquency	888	15.00	40.00	21.6959	5.9064	1.533	.082
Family Problems	888	14.00	31.00	21.6554	3.9814	.095	.082
Magnitude of Damage	888	.00	60000.00	6637.02	11497.7643	2.501	.082
Enuresis	888	1.00	2.00	1.0912	.2881	2.844	.082
Pathology	888	27.99	95.71	50.0000	10.0000	1.646	.082
Peer Problems	888	15.00	37.00	24.8345	5.1582	.343	.082
Recidivism	315	1.00	2.00	1.8571	.3505	-2.051	.137
School Problems	888	6.00	17.00	11.2264	3.0263	.069	.082
Social Skills	888	34.89	74.78	50.0000	10.0000	.787	.082

CHAPTER FOUR
ANALYSIS OF FEDERAL EMERGENCY MANAGEMENT AGENCY FORMS
(Fineman, 1997a, 1997b, 1997c)

Introduction

The purpose of this chapter is to examine the stability and psychometric structure of the Federal Emergency Management Agency (FEMA) firesetting forms. Each of the three instruments (Fineman, 1997a, 1997b, 1997c) will be assessed separately.

FEMA's Fire Risk Interview Forms (Fineman, 1997a, 1997b, 1997c)

The Fire Risk Interview Forms (Fineman, 1997a, 1997b, 1997c) are meant to assess family contextual variables considered to be related to recurrent firesetting. The instruments also are meant to gain information that might guide fire service personnel in focusing the content for the juvenile during educational interventions.

When taking the Fire Risk Interview Forms, a person is asked to indicate their perception of the statements given. The higher a juvenile's score, the more they are thought to be at risk for firesetting recidivism. The lower a juvenile's score, the less they are thought to be likely to engage in recidivistic firesetting behaviors.

To date, no normative data have been compiled for the FEMA Fire Risk Interview Forms. Nonetheless, the Federal Emergency Management Agency praises the forms for their predictive purposes in identifying recidivists amongst firesetters (FEMA, 1995). FEMA also has suggested that the interview forms be used to teach fire service personnel strategies for educating firesetters and their families. However, because no normative information has been found on the stability or truthfulness of the inventories, classification of individuals using these instruments may be ill-advised.

Construction of the inventories. In creating the Fire Risk Interview Forms (1997a, 1997b, 1997c), Fineman based their construction on two specific assumptions. First, it was assumed that juvenile firesetters could be clustered into two mutually exclusive categories, those who are recidivists versus those who are not. Second, it was assumed that curiosity firesetters are not likely to be recidivists. However, it is not clear that either assertion is valid when examining juvenile firesetters. Moreover, item transparency may be a concern, in that it is likely that curiosity firesetters who were inclined to become recidivists may be attuned to answering these questions in socially-desirable ways and would not be motivated to answer the questions truthfully.

To document the psychometric efficacy of these instruments, it was judged important to establish some estimates of scale reliabilities. Reliability serves as a necessary but insufficient prerequisite to validity. Nunnally (1994) suggests that in pilot or early research studies, a reliability estimates of .70 is sufficient. However, in later research and policy making studies, reliability coefficients should exceed .80. Given the exploratory character of these analyses, Nunnally's lower guideline might be justified in performing the following reliability estimates. However, given the importance of decisions that may be linked to these instruments, the higher coefficient will be applied.

FEMA's (1997a) Family Fire Risk Interview Form

The Family Fire Risk Interview Form (Fineman, 1997a; see Appendix A) is the first form completed by a family during a fire service personnel interview. The interviewer is responsible for reading aloud questions from the interview form in a semi-structured format. The Family Fire Risk Inventory may be self-administered, though because of literacy issues many fire personnel prefer to read the questions aloud to families and to fill in responses for them. Although it has been used primarily with children and adolescents, the items on the Family Fire Risk Interview are presumed to be comprehensible to most elementary school students.

Most questions on the interview form are answered by the parent/guardian, but juveniles are able to interject their beliefs during the interview (Spurlin, 1999, personal communication). Completion time for the 65-question interview form is approximately 30 minutes.

Administration and Scoring

The Family Fire Risk Interview Form includes 65 questions, some of which are in Likert Scale format, some of which are forced-choice, and some of which are open-ended. Those with Likert scales range from 1 (Rarely to never) to 3 (Frequently). Parents were required to answer statements such as [my child has] "learning problems at school," [my child is] "physically violent," and [my child has] "curiosity about fire."

Psychometric Qualities of the Family Fire Risk Interview Form Scales

The Family Fire Risk Interview Form contains 9 scales: (1) health history scale, (2) family structure issues, (3) peer issues, (4) school issues, (5) behavior issues, (6) fire history, (7) presence of crisis or trauma, (8) characteristics of firestart, and (9) general observations.

Health history scale. Six questions on the health history scale were meant to assess concerns regarding juveniles' physical and mental stability. Two questions were related to operating smoke detectors in the home. The form included forced-choice statements with responses categorized as one (low risk of recidivism) or two (high risk of recidivism).

In order to perform an item analysis for this scale several questions had to be inverted to be oriented in common with the other questions on the scale (items 4, 8, and 9). Assessment of internal consistency of the health history scale on the Family Fire Risk Interview Form using the MCAIN data revealed an unacceptable level of reliability, with a Cronbach's alpha of .57.

Family structure issues. Family structure issues were addressed through 12 forced-choice statements and Likert-format statements, and were meant to assess concerns regarding the stability of the family. Three statements did not fit this Likert-scale format, but were forced on the instrument into the same child and parent scoring system. Items also included statements regarding the involvement of parents with their children with respect to fulfillment of needs, use of discipline, and the presence of over-protection. The form included statements with responses ranging from one (low stability in home) to five (high stability in family).

In order to perform an item analysis for this scale several questions had to be inverted to be oriented in common with the other questions on the scale (items 10, 14, 16). Unlike the rest of the Family Fire Risk Inventory, a higher score on this scale is an indication of greater stability (whereas theoretically, a higher score is expected to be an indication of dysfunction and recidivism). After questions were inverted, assessment of internal consistency of the family structures issues scale of the Family Fire Risk Interview Form using the MCAIN data revealed a poor to fair level of reliability, with a Cronbach's alpha of .66.

Peer issues. Peer issues were addressed through forced-choice statements about interactions with juveniles, and were meant to assess concerns regarding fighting, getting picked on by others, and the influence of peers. This scale included five statements. No items had to be inverted to analyze this scale. Assessment of internal consistency of the peer issues scale of the Family Fire Risk Interview Form using the MCAIN data revealed a fair level of reliability, with a Cronbach's alpha of .68.

School issues. School issues were addressed through forced-choice and Likert-scale statements about the juvenile's academic record, and were meant to assess concerns regarding fighting at school, learning disabilities, and the influence of teachers. This scale included five statements.

In order to perform an item analysis for this scale several questions had to be inverted to be oriented in common with the other questions on the scale (items 28, 29, 30). Unlike the rest of the Family Fire Risk Inventory, a higher score on this scale is an indication of greater stability (whereas theoretically, a higher score is expected to be an indication of dysfunction and recidivism). After items were inverted, assessment of internal consistency of the school issues scale using the MCAIN data revealed a fair level of reliability, with a Cronbach's alpha of .74.

Behavior issues. Behavior issues were addressed through six forced-choice statements about delinquent-type involvement, and were meant to assess concerns regarding difficulty with authority. Respondents and their families were given statements such as "Has your child ever lied excessively," or "does your child frequently say no when they are asked to do something?" This scale was one of the strongest scales with respect to face validity and stability. Assessment of internal consistency of the behavior issues scale using the MCAIN data revealed an acceptable level of reliability, with a Cronbach's alpha of .82.

Fire history. Juveniles' fire histories were addressed through seven forced-choice and Likert-format statements, and were meant to assess concerns about using fire, mimicking fire behaviors of others in family, and previous interacting with fire. The form included statements with responses ranging from one (low involvement with firesetting) to four (high involvement with firesetting), as well as forced choice items.

In order to perform an item analysis for this scale several questions had to be inverted to be oriented in common with the other questions on the scale (items 38, 39, 40). Unlike the rest of the Family Fire Risk Inventory, a higher score on this scale is an indication of greater stability (whereas theoretically, a higher score is expected to be an indication of dysfunction and recidivism). Also some of the items needed to be altered from a forced-choice format to a Likert-like scale (items 38, 39, and 40 were changed from 1 = acceptable and 2 = poor to 1 = acceptable and 4 = poor). After items were inverted and reformatted, assessment of internal consistency for the fire history scale using the MCAIN data revealed an acceptable level of reliability, with a Cronbach's alpha of .84.

Presence of crisis or trauma. Presence of crisis or trauma was addressed through three forced-choice statements that were meant to assess concerns regarding involvement with stressful events, including presence of medical illness, witnessing domestic violence, witnessing physical aggression between others (including parents), and excessive anger control problems at home or in school. The form included statements with responses ranging from 1 (low presence of crisis) to 5 (high presence of crisis). Assessment of internal consistency of the presence of crisis or trauma scale using the MCAIN data revealed a fair level of reliability, with a Cronbach's alpha of .74.

Characteristics of firestart. Characteristics of firestart were addressed through 15 open-ended statements about the acts that led up to and included the firesetting event. Respondents and their families were given statements such as "Where was the fire set or where did the firesetting occur?," and "How did the child get material to start the fire or engage in firesetting?."

In order to perform an item analysis for this scale, several questions were removed, due to the open-ended nature of the response (items 47, 50, 51, and 52). Also, some of the items needed to be altered from a Likert-like scale to a forced choice format (items 46, 48, 49, 54, and 61). After items were inverted, assessment of internal consistency of the characteristics of firestart using the MCAIN data revealed a fair level of reliability, with a Cronbach's alpha of .71.

General observations. General observations about the juvenile and their family were addressed through four open-ended statements about the manner of participants during the interview. Interviewers were asked to review the male and female caregivers' actions toward the child. Internal consistency for the general observations scale was poor, with a Cronbach's alpha of .65 (see Table 10).

Table 10

Reliability Estimates for Family Fire Risk Interview Form (Fineman, 1997a)

Scale	alpha
Health History Scale	.57
Family Structure Issues Scale	.66
Peer Issues Scale	.68
School Issues Scale	.74
Behavior Issues Scale	.82
Fire History Scale	.84
Presence of Crisis or Trauma Scale	.74
Characteristics of Firestart Scale	.71
General Observations Scale	.65

Only two of the nine FEMA Family Fire Risk Inventory scales, Fire History and Behavior Issues, were found to have sufficient reliability estimates (Nunnally, 1994) for making judgments about the juveniles and their family.

Test-Retest Reliability

The Family Fire Risk Inventory was administered for a second time to 12 female recidivists and 22 male recidivists from the original sample who returned to Fire Stop due to the setting of at least a second fire. The second administration took place approximately three to four months after the first. During the second administration, participants were told that the author was interested in how their responses on the test might vary over time. Participants were explicitly instructed not to try to remember how they had responded previously.

In order to gage the internal consistency of the Family Fire Risk Inventory, Pearson product moment correlations were computed separately for males and females in both samples. Product-moment correlations for all scales were found to range from .64 to .70 for both males and females. Product-moment correlations were computed between the first and second administrations with limited reliable results (r = .62).

The Revised Form of the Family Fire Risk Inventory

The author believed that higher levels of internal consistency were possible with a reduction of items. Based on the original attitudes acquired from the participants (n = 888), a second form of the Family Fire Risk Inventory was constructed. The Revised Form of the Family Fire Risk Inventory included 50 of the original 65-items from the original FEMA Family Fire Risk Inventory (Fineman, 1997a). It constitutes a refinement of the original form, and is to serve as a convenience in scoring when compared with the original form (see Table 11). Because of the need for information needed for purposes of identifying abuse or neglect, some questions were included in the revised draft that lowered the alpha of the instrument (see questions 26, 31, 32, 34, 38, 43, 44, and 45).

Table 11

Items Chosen for the Revised Version of FEMA Family Fire Risk Interview Form

Item	Corrected Item-Total r	Alpha if Item is Deleted
02. Does your child take any medication for impulsivity?	.5017	.5021
03. Has your child been diagnosed with an impulse control condition?	.4871	.5002
04. Is your child not receiving counseling for issues they may be facing?	.5138	.5131
06. Are there any smokers in your home?	.4995	.4789
07. Are there operating smoke detectors in your home?	.5564	.5877
08. Were there operating smoke detectors at the time of this incident?	.5417	.5428
09. Have you rented or owned at your present location for more than 5 years?	.6678	.6435
11. Is the mother ever unavailable to the child when he/she needs you?	.6571	.6571
12. Is the father ever unavailable to the child when he/she needs you?	.6623	.6780
13. Do you not spend enough time with your child?	.6546	.6631
14. Are there significant conflicts between this child and members of the family?	.6366	.6121
15. Do you not have adequate control over your child?	.6620	.6914
16. Do you ignore bad behavior when your child is badly behaved?	.6407	.6521
17. Do you discipline your child differently each time they are badly behaved?	.6553	.6353
18. Is there a history of emotional abuse in the family?	.6344	.6326
19. Is there a history of physical abuse in the family?	.7344	.7593
20. Is there a history of sexual abuse in the family?	.4741	.5220
21. Does your child interact poorly with peers?	.5963	.5842
22. Does your child get into fights frequently?	.5381	.5267
23. Does your child get picked on by other children?	.6840	.6900
24. Does your child frequently play alone rather than with other children?	.6808	.6831
25. Do you think your child's friends are a bad influence?	.6801	.6489
26. Has your child been held back a grade or more in school?	.8796	.8072
27. Does your child have difficulties academically with school?	.6993	.6331
29. Does your child have any special educational learning needs?	.6798	.6842
30. Have there been any discipline problems at school?	.7213	.7751
31. Has your child been in trouble outside of school?	.8813	.9038
32. Does your child frequently say no when asked to do something?	.8763	.9038
33. Has your child ever stolen or shoplifted?	.8901	.7422
34. Has your child lied excessively?	.8841	.9129
35. Has your child ever used drugs/alcohol/inhalants?	.9187	.7939
36. Has your child ever beat up or hurt others?	.8969	.8505
37. Was the child unsupervised when the fire occurred?	.8217	.8384
38. Are matches or lighters readily available to the child?	.8401	.8754
41. Is your child curious about fire?	.8108	.7243

Table 11 (continued)

Items Chosen for the Revised Version of FEMA Family Fire Risk Interview Form

Item	Corrected Item-Total r	Alpha if Item is Deleted
42. Has your child ever used fire inappropriately prior to this event?	.8301	.8222
43. Was there much damage caused by the fires started before this one?	.8034	.8398
44. Has anything bad happened in the family or your child's life in the past year?	.8072	.8903
45. Has there been an ongoing (chronic) crisis in your life or in the family?	.7970	.8530
49. Did the fire occur in an occupied structure or close to others?	.6599	.7346
54. Did the child tell the truth about their involvement?	.6651	.6331
55. Did the child act alone?	.6654	.6489
56. Was the child pressured into firesetting by their peers?	.7032	.7275
57. Did the child respond to the firesetting as if it was humorous?	.7290	.7291
58. Does the child believe that fire has spiritual qualities or powers?	.6965	.6285
59. Is there an impulsive quality to the child's firesetting?	.6915	.5853
60. Did you respond to the fire by physically punishing or yelling at the child?	.6908	.6408
62. Does the mother act concerned with the child?	.6874	.6748
63. Does the father act concerned with the child?	.4256	.6293

FEMA's (1997b) Juvenile Fire Risk Interview Form

The Juvenile Fire Risk Interview Form (Fineman, 1997b; see Appendix B) is the second form completed by a family during a fire service personnel interview. The interviewer is responsible for reading aloud questions from the interview form in a semi-structured format (Spurlin, 1999, personal communication). Completion time for the 57-question interview form is approximately 30 minutes. The Juvenile Fire Risk Interview Form may be self-administered, though because of literacy issues many fire personnel prefer to read the questions aloud to juveniles and to fill in responses for them. Although it has been used primarily with children and adolescents, the items on the Juvenile Fire Risk Interview Form should be comprehensible to most elementary school students.

Administration and Scoring

The Juvenile Fire Risk Interview Form includes 57 questions, some of which are in Likert-scale format, some of which are forced-choice, and some of which are open-ended. Those with Likert-scales range from 1 (Rarely to never) to 3 (Frequently). Juveniles are required to answer statements such as [I have] "learning problems at school," [I am] "physically violent," and [I have] "curiosity about fire."

Psychometric Properties of the Juvenile Fire Risk Interview Form Scales

The Juvenile Fire Risk Interview Form contains seven scales: (1) school issues, (2) peer issues, (3) behavior issues, (4) family issues, (5) crisis or trauma, (6) fire history, and (7) characteristics of firestart.

School issues. School issues were addressed through four forced-choice statements about the juvenile's academic record, and were meant to assess concerns regarding fighting at school, learning disabilities, and the influence of teachers. In order to perform an item analysis for this scale several questions had to be coded in a way similar to the other questions on the scale (items 3 and 4). Unlike the rest of the Juvenile Fire Risk Inventory, a higher score on this scale is an indication of greater stability (whereas theoretically, a higher score is expected to be an indication of dysfunction and recidivism). After statements were inverted, assessment of internal consistency for the school issues scale using the MCAIN data revealed a fair level of reliability, with a Cronbach's alpha of .78.

Peer issues. Peer issues were addressed through five forced-choice statements about interactions with juveniles, and were meant to assess concerns regarding fighting with peers, getting picked on by others, and the influence of peers. In order to perform an item analysis for this scale, several questions had to be inverted to be coded in a way similar to the other questions on the scale (items 5 and 7). Assessment of internal consistency for the peer issues scale using the MCAIN data revealed an unacceptable level of reliability, with a Cronbach's alpha of .56.

Behavior issues. Behavior issues were addressed through forced-choice statements about delinquent-type involvement, and were meant to assess concerns regarding difficulty with authority. Respondents were given statements such as "Has your child ever lied excessively," or "does your child frequently say no when they are asked to do something?" In order to perform an item analysis for this scale, one question had to be inverted to be coded similar to the other questions on the scale (item 11). This scale included six statements, and was one of the strongest scales with respect to face validity and stability. Assessment of internal consistency for the behavior issues scale using the MCAIN data revealed an acceptable level of reliability, with a Cronbach's alpha of .83.

Family structure issues. Family structure issues were addressed through 14 forced-choice statements and were meant to assess concerns regarding the stability of the family, and the involvement of parents with their children with respect to fulfillment of needs, use of discipline, and the presence of over-protection. The form included statements with responses ranging from 1 (low stability in home) to 5 (high stability in juvenile). Three statements did not fit this Likert-scale format, but were forced on the instrument into the same child and parent scoring system (items 16, 25, and 26).

In order to perform an item analysis for this scale several questions had to be inverted to be oriented in common with the other questions on the scale (items 17, 20, 24, 25, and 26). Unlike the rest of the Juvenile Fire Risk Interview Form, a higher score on this scale was an indication of greater stability (whereas theoretically, a higher score is expected to be an indication of dysfunction and recidivism). After questions were inverted, assessment of internal consistency for the family structures issues scale using the MCAIN data revealed an unacceptable level of reliability, with a Cronbach's alpha of .54.

Presence of crisis or trauma. Presence of crisis or trauma was addressed through three forced-choice statements and were meant to assess concerns regarding involvement with stressful events, including the presence of medical illness, witnessing domestic violence, witnessing physical aggression between others (including parents), and excessive anger control problems at home or in school. Assessment of internal consistency for the presence of crisis or trauma scale using the MCAIN data revealed a fair level of reliability, with a Cronbach's alpha of .73.

Fire history. Juveniles' fire histories were addressed through seven forced-choice and Likert-format statements that were meant to assess concerns about using fire, mimicking fire behaviors of others in the family, and previously interacting with fire. The form included statements with responses ranging from 1 (low involvement with firesetting) to 4 (high involvement with firesetting), as well as forced choice items.

In order to perform an item analysis for this scale one question had to be inverted to be oriented in common with the other questions on the scale (item 39). Also some of the items needed to be altered from a Likert-like scale to a forced-choice format (items 36 and 37 were changed from 1 or 2 = acceptable (1) and 3 or 4 = poor (2)). After questions were inverted, assessment of internal consistency for the fire history scale using the MCAIN data revealed an acceptable level of reliability, with a Cronbach's alpha of .83.

Characteristics of firestart. Characteristics of firestart were addressed through 13 open-ended statements about the acts that led up to and included the firesetting event. Respondents were given statements such as "Where was the fire set?," "Where did the firesetting occur?," and "How did the child get material to start the fire or engage in firesetting?." This scale included 13 statements.

In order to perform an item analysis for this scale, several questions were removed, due to the open-ended nature of the response (items 41, 43). Also, some of the items needed to be altered from a Likert-like scale to a forced choice format (items 40, 42, 46, 48, and 49, and 52). After questions were inverted, assessment of internal consistency for the characteristics of firestart scale using the MCAIN data revealed a poor level of reliability, with a Cronbach's alpha of .51 (see Table 12).

Only two of the nine FEMA Juvenile Fire Risk Inventory scales, Fire History and Behavior Issues, were found to have sufficient reliability estimates (Nunnally, 1994) for making judgments about the juveniles and their family.

Table 12

Reliability Estimates for Juvenile Fire Risk Interview Form (Fineman, 1997b)

Scale	alpha
School Issues Scale	.78
Peer Issues Scale	.56
Behavior Issues Scale	.83
Family Structure Issues Scale	.54
Presence of Crisis or Trauma Scale	.73
Fire History Scale	.83
Characteristics of Firestart Scale	.51

Test-Retest Reliability

The Juvenile Fire Risk Interview Form was administered for a second time to 12 female recidivists and 22 male recidivists from the original sample who had been referred to the MCAIN Fire Stop program for a second fire. The second administration took place approximately 3 to 4 months after the first. During the second administration, participants were told that the author was interested in how their responses on the test might vary over time. Participants were explicitly instructed not to try to remember how they had responded previously. Product-moment correlations were computed between the first and second administrations with limited reliable results ($r = .59$).

The Revised Form of the Juvenile Fire Risk Inventory

The author believed that higher levels of internal consistency were possible with a reduction of items. Based on the original attitudes acquired from the participants ($n = 888$), a second form of the Juvenile Fire Risk Interview Form was constructed. Using the means, standard deviations, and corrected item-total correlations, 52 items were used (see Table 13). The Revised Form of the Juvenile Fire Risk Interview Form included 52 of the original 57 items from the original FEMA Juvenile Fire Risk Interview Form (Fineman, 1997b). It constitutes a refinement of the original form, and is to serve as a convenience in scoring.

FEMA's (1997c) Parent Fire Risk Questionnaire

The Parent Fire Risk Questionnaire (Fineman, 1997c; see Appendix C) is meant to assess both family and juvenile contextual variables considered to be related to recurrent firesetting. The instrument also is meant to gain information that might guide fire service personnel in focusing the content for the juvenile during educational interventions.

The Parent Fire Risk Questionnaire (Fineman, 1997c) is the final form completed by a parent during a fire service personnel interview. The parent is responsible for answering all 116 statements, which are constructed in a 3-point Likert-scale format. The Parent Fire Risk Questionnaire is essentially self-administering, though due to literacy concerns many fire personnel prefer to read the questions aloud to parents and to fill in their responses for them. For the purposes of this study, questionnaires were completed by the parent. Completion time for this interview form is approximately 20 minutes.

Table 13

Items Chosen for the Revised Version of FEMA Juvenile Fire Risk Inventory

Item	Corrected Item-Total r	Alpha If Item Is Deleted
1. Do you dislike school/learning?	.8328	.6793
2. Do you ignore your teachers most of the time?	.7589	.6733
3. Have there been any problems with your school performance?	.7609	.6120
4. Have you gotten in trouble at school?	.8283	.6456
5. Do you get along with most of your friends?	.6080	.6160
6. Do you get picked on?	.6501	.6287
7. Do you have as many friends as you want?	.5039	.6230
8. Do you want to be alone or with other kids?	.6190	.6439
9. Do you think your friends are a bad influence on you?	.5436	.6643
10. Do you get in trouble frequently outside of school?	.7666	.6326
11. Do you usually do things you are asked to do?	.8114	.6142
12. Have you ever stolen or shoplifted?	.8043	.6201
13. Do you lie frequently?	.8056	.6219
14. Have you ever used drugs/alcohol/inhalants?	.8128	.6255
15. Have you ever beat up or hurt others?	.7843	.6139
16. Do you like going home?	.6052	.6255
17. Do you get along with your mother?	.6234	.6028
18. Do you fight or argue with your mother?	.5701	.6255
19. Are you afraid of your mother?	.4823	.6792
20. Do you get along with your father?	.5838	.6453
21. Do you fight or argue with your father?	.5610	.6333
22. Are you afraid of your father?	.5042	.6108
23. Do your mother and father fight?	.4435	.6652
24. Do you get along with your brothers and sisters?	.5364	.6547
25. Do you see your mom as much as you like?	.4930	.6979
26. Do you see your dad as much as you like?	.4970	.6941
27. What do you do that gets you in trouble at home?	.6138	.6545
28. Do you get punished when you get in trouble?	.4774	.6232
30. Within the past year has anything bad happened in your life?	.6033	.6576
31. Has there been an ongoing (chronic) crisis/problem in your life?	.5973	.5926
33. Do you like to look at fires for long periods of time?	.8021	.6100
42. Did you get the (above igniter) to start the fire from home?	.7955	.5884
44. Did you set the fire in an occupied structure or near others?	.5769	.6343
45. Did you intend to set the fire?	.4359	.7074
47. Did you drink or take any drugs before during or after the fire?	.4859	.6878
49. Did your parents punish you for setting the fire?	.4407	.6921
50. Did the fire you started make you happy or make you laugh?	.4115	.7044

Administration and Scoring

The Parent Fire Risk Questionnaire includes eight scales. The questionnaire includes 116 questions. The Likert-scale statements range from 1 (Rarely to never) to 3 (Frequently), parents were required to answer statements such as [my child has] "learning problems at school," [my child is] "physically violent," and [my child has] "curiosity about fire."

Psychometric Properties of the Parent Fire Risk Questionnaire Scales

The Parent Fire Risk Questionnaire contains eight scales: (1) school issues, (2) health history scale, (3) peer issues, (4) behavior issues, (5) somatic and psychiatric issues, (6) fire history scale, (7) family structure issues, and (8) general pathology scale.

School issues. School issues were addressed through 11 Likert-scale statements about the juvenile's academic record, and were meant to assess concerns regarding fighting at school, learning disabilities, and the influence of teachers. In order to perform an item analysis for this scale several statements had to be inverted to be organized in a way that was theoretically similar with the other statements on the scale (items 8, 9, and 10). After statements were inverted, assessment of internal consistency for the school issues scale using the MCAIN data revealed a fair level of reliability, with a Cronbach's alpha of .64.

Health history issues. The health history scale addressed concerns regarding the child's physical and mental stability through 19 statements. The form included Likert-scale statements with responses ranging from 1 (low risk of recidivism) to 3 (high risk of recidivism).

In order to perform an item analysis for this scale several questions had to be inverted to be oriented in common with the other questions on the scale (items 18, 19, 20, 26 and 30).

Assessment of internal consistency for the health history issues scale using the MCAIN data revealed an unacceptable level of reliability, with a Cronbach's alpha of .35.

Peer issues. Peer issues were addressed through 12 forced-choice statements about interactions with juveniles, and included statements that were meant to assess concerns regarding fighting with peers, getting picked on by others, and the influence of peers. Several items had to be inverted to assess the reliability of this scale (items 37, 38, 41, and 42). Assessment of internal consistency for the peer issues scale using the MCAIN data revealed an acceptable level of reliability, with a Cronbach's alpha of .84.

Behavior issues. Behavior issues were addressed through forced-choice statements about delinquent-type involvement, and were meant to assess concerns regarding difficulty with authority. Respondents' parents were given statements such as "Has your child ever lied excessively?," or "does your child frequently say no when they are asked to do something?" This scale included 19 statements, and was one of the strongest scales with respect to face validity and stability. Assessment of internal consistency for the behavior issues scale using the MCAIN data revealed an acceptable level of reliability, with a Cronbach's alpha of .94.

Somatic and psychiatric issues. Somatic and psychiatric issues were addressed through Likert-scale statements that were meant to assess concerns regarding the psychiatric stability of the juvenile, as well as any somatic problems they might have. The form included statements with responses ranging from 1 (high stability) to 3 (low stability). This scale included 18 statements. Assessment of internal consistency for the somatic and psychiatric issues scale using the MCAIN data revealed a fair level of reliability, with a Cronbach's alpha of .79.

Fire history. The juvenile's fire history was addressed through 12 Likert-format statements that were meant to assess concerns regarding the using of fire, mimicking fire behaviors of others in family, and previous interactions with fire. The form included statements with responses ranging from 1 (low involvement with firesetting) to 3 (high involvement with firesetting), as well as forced choice items.

In order to perform an item analysis for this scale several questions had to be inverted to be oriented in common with the other questions on the scale (items 84 and 89). After statements were inverted, assessment of internal consistency for the fire history scale using the MCAIN data revealed a fair level of reliability, with a Cronbach's alpha of .64.

Family structure issues. Family structure issues were addressed through Likert-scale statements that were meant to assess concerns regarding the stability of the family, and the involvement of parents with their children with respect to fulfillment of needs, use of discipline, and the presence of over-protection. The form included statements with responses ranging from 1 (high stability in home) to 3 (low stability in family). This scale included 14 statements.

In order to perform an item analysis for this scale several questions had to be inverted to be oriented in common with the other questions on the scale (items 103 and 104). After statements were inverted, assessment of internal consistency for the family structure issues scale using the MCAIN data revealed a fair level of reliability, with a Cronbach's alpha of .70.

General pathology. General pathology about the juvenile was addressed through Likert-scale statements. This scale included 10 statements, such as juvenile has "unusual fantasies" or "bizarre or irrational speech." Assessment of internal consistency for the general pathology scale using the MCAIN data revealed an acceptable level of reliability, with a Cronbach's alpha of .86 (see Table 14).

Table 14

Reliability Estimates for Parent Fire Risk Questionnaire (Fineman, 1997c)

Scale	Alpha
School Issues Scale	.64
Health History Scale	.35
Peer Issues Scale	.84
Behavior Issues Scale	.94
Somatic and Psychiatric Issues Scale	.79
Fire History Scale	.64
Family Structure Issues Scale	.70
General Pathology Scale	.86

Test-Retest Reliability

The Parent Fire Risk Questionnaire was administered for a second time to 12 female recidivists and 22 male recidivists from the original sample who were referred back to the Fire Stop program following a second fire event. The second administration took place approximately 3 to 4 months after the first. During the second administration, participants were told that the author was interested in how their responses on the test might vary over time. Participants were explicitly instructed not to try to remember how they had responded previously.

Only three of the nine FEMA Juvenile Fire Risk Inventory scales, Peer Issues, Behavior Issues, and General Pathology, were found to have sufficient reliability estimates (Nunnally, 1994) for making judgments about the juveniles and their family.

Conclusions for FEMA Fire Risk Interview Forms (Fineman, 1997a, 1997b, 1997c)

The Fire Risk Interview Forms lack any relevant reviews of criterion-related validity or content validity. Another problem that could concern researchers was the sole use of theory in creating the instrument, with no discussion of any pilot data (see Federal Emergency Management Agency, 1996). Although criterion-related validity would have been reached, construct validity may not have been addressed. Perhaps FEMA is simply studying the social desirability of traits for firesetters, not identities related to recidivist tendencies.

Construct validity and content validity are concerns for the instruments. It seems logical that a group of characteristics could be historically-defined as being related either to curiosity firesetting or a form of recidivist, pathological firesetting. However, few studies have been undertaken with other types of questionnaires in order to validate the criteria present on the inventory. It would be very difficult to identify whether or not the questionnaires contain the necessary domains needed to predict recidivism and identify the type of firesetter.

Problems with social desirability would indicate that content validity may be an issue for the Fire Risk Interview Forms. As such, further studies pairing observational data with questionnaire results should be performed. In future analyses of the interview forms, an empirical check on the relationship between social desirability response set and an individual's score should be made. At this point in its construction, such analyses could not be completed.

However, based on the confidential nature of the results and the range with which individuals responded to the statements, the author believes that participants felt free to answer honestly.

CHAPTER FIVE
RESULTS

Juvenile firesetters represent a population of significant social concern; however, current understanding of this group is limited. The purpose of this study was to explore the relationships of individual and environmental variables to firesetting in juveniles ages 3 years to 18 years of age. The theoretical context that describes this population is aligned with Jessor and Jessor's problem behavior theory (Jessor & Jessor, 1984). Juvenile firesetting reflects an example of atypical psychosocial development. The present study focuses on developmental factors that relate to the initiation or continuation of juvenile firesetting.

Hypotheses of the Study

This study investigated the following hypotheses:

1. The presence of enuresis and cruelty to animals in juvenile firesetters will be related to recidivistic firesetting.
2. The magnitude of fire damages will be predicted by individual and environmental factors, with environmental factors being found to be better predictors.
3. The presence of recidivism will be predicted by individual and environmental factors, with individual factors being found to be better predictors.
4. The typology of the juvenile firesetter will be predicted by individual and environmental factors, with environmental factors being found to be better predictors.
5. A developmental pattern will be identified with juvenile firesetters, with juvenile firesetters ages 3 years to 10 years being predicted more with environmental factors, while juvenile firesetters over the age of 10 years being predicted more with individual factors.

6. Firesetting in children ages 3 to 6 years is more likely to result in greater destructiveness to property and loss of life than the firesetting of any other age group.

Examination of Scales

Initially, it was believed that both individual and environmental variables would need to be examined in order to predict certain characteristics of juvenile firesetting; such as the magnitude of fire damage, recidivistic behaviors, and the type of firesetter. With this individual-environmental dichotomy in mind, three individual scales (aggression, delinquency, and externalization of emotions) and three environmental scales (family problems, school problems, and peer problems) were established. Questions were organized from the FEMA juvenile firesetter forms (Fineman, 1997c). Individual items were matched to the defined concepts organized by both the individual and environmental principles to create scales.

Table 15

Reliability Estimates for Individual Scales and Environmental Scales

	Cronbach's Alpha	items on scale
Individual scales		
Affinity toward aggression	.59	14 items
Delinquency	.90	16 items
Externalization of emotions	.79	27 items
Environmental scales		
Family problems	.57	14 items
School problems	.71	6 items
Peer problems	.67	12 items

When examining the six scales, the externalization of emotions and delinquency scales appear to show satisfactory reliability. However, examination of bivariate relationships revealed all scales to be colinear; all of the scales correlated with one another significantly at the .001 level. Given that neither the FEMA scales (see Chapter 4) nor the hypothesized scales possessed sufficient psychometric integrity as configured, the author elected to use an exploratory data analysis to identify a set of stable variables that could assist in further understanding the hypotheses under study.

For the purposes of the present study, analyses were limited to the Parent Fire Risk Questionnaire (Fineman, 1997c). The FEMA Parent Fire Risk Questionnaire (Fineman, 1997c) holds the advantage of a single format for all items; this is not the case with the other FEMA instruments. It is perhaps because of this attribute that the Parent Fire Risk Questionnaire was found to have the strongest reliability estimates and item transparency appeared to be less of an issue. Items on this scale were subject to exploratory data analysis using SPSS Version 9.0.

Exploratory Factor Analysis

Prior to the exploratory factor analysis, the author examined the descriptive characteristics of each item. Any item that showed 80% or more responses on one choice were eliminated. The result was the elimination of 15 items.

Principal component analysis was performed on the 101 of the 116 items of the FEMA Parent Fire Risk Questionnaire (Fineman, 1997c). Principal component analysis was performed with no limits on the number of factors to be elicited or the number of iterations necessary to yield the factors. Determination of the final factor structure also was guided by an examination of the Scree plot of eigenvalues that revealed a break between the second and third eigenvalues (an indication to limit the number of factors to three). Using a critical eigenvalue greater than 1.0 also suggested a 3-factor solution. A maximum likelihood chi-square test of fit also was performed, which indicated that a 3-factor model would maximize the determinant of the residual correlation matrix.

Preliminary eigenvalues were observed to examine whether unidimensionality of the model was a concern. Unidimensionality was not found to be a problem, in that the second eigenvalue was not found to be five times smaller than the first factor. With 3 factors, it was possible to explain 40% of the instrument's variance.

The iterated principal factor analysis showed that a convergence criterion was satisfied within three iterations. A principal component analysis was performed based on three factors. Squared multiple correlations were used to estimate initial communalities. Shared variance was estimated by communalities, which indicated that there was some relationship found within the matrix. Components for each of the three factors only loaded on one factor, an indication of the stability of the factors.

Jessor's Theory Revisited: Pathology, Delinquency, and Social Skills

It would appear that the resulting factor structure is consonant with Jessor's theory of problem behavior. Jessor outlines three principal individual components that have been identified throughout the literature in examining problem behaviors: the presence of pathology, social skills, and delinquent tendencies (see Rachal et al., 1980).

Factor one: Pathology. As a factor under consideration, pathology was identified using six items. Pathology was meant to assess concerns regarding individual psychopathology, and included items such as [juvenile has] "unusual fantasies," "strange thought patterns," and "bizarre and irrational speech." Each statement related to pathology with responses ranging from 1 (low pathology) to 3 (high pathology) (see Table 16). Internal consistency for the pathology scale was acceptable and high, with an estimated Cronbach's alpha of .87.

Factor two: Delinquency. Delinquency was identified as any behavior that was bothersome to caregivers (e.g., highly stubborn behavior, lying, truancy, running away from home) or that inflicted harm or property loss on other (vandalism, theft, violent acts). Delinquency included items such as child "expresses anger by hurting self or something he likes," "cruel to animals," and "steals." Each statement related to delinquency with responses ranging from 1 (low levels of delinquency) to 3 (high levels of delinquency) (see Table 16). Internal consistency for the delinquency scale was acceptable and high, with an estimated Cronbach's alpha of .92.

Factor three: Social skills. Social skills were identified as being a measure of individual difficulty in interacting with others in appropriate ways, and included 18 items (see Table 16). The factor included items such as [child has] "extreme mood swings," temper tantrums," and [child is] "cruel to other children." Each statement related to social skills with responses ranging from 1 (low social skills) to 3 (high social skills). Internal consistency for the social skills scale was acceptable and high, with an estimated Cronbach's alpha of .88.

Revised Hypotheses under Investigation

Five sets of analyses were carried out to test the five revised hypotheses under consideration. They are as follows:

1. The presence of enuresis and cruelty to animals in juvenile firesetters will be related to recidivistic firesetting,
2. The magnitude of fire damages will be predicted by levels of pathology, social skills, delinquency, as well as the age of the firesetter,
3. The presence of recidivism will be predicted by levels of pathology, social skills, delinquency, as well as the age of the firesetter,
4. The typology of the juvenile firesetter will be predicted by levels of pathology, social skills, delinquency, as well as the age, race, and sex of the firesetter, and
5. A developmental pattern will be predicted with firesetters by examining levels of pathology, social skills, and delinquency.

Table 16

Related factor loadings for the FEMA Parent Fire Risk Questionnaire (loadings less than .50 excluded)

Item	Pathology	Delinquency	Limited Sociability
Bizarre and irrational speech	.82		
Unusual fantasies	.80		
Strange thought patterns	.79		
Strange quality about child	.73		
Out of touch with reality	.62		
Severe depression/withdrawal	.50		
Has been in trouble with police		.75	
Sexual activity with others		.72	
Uses drugs or alcohol		.65	
Cruel to animals		.66	
Steals		.62	
Expresses anger by hurting self/something likes		.54	
Is a loner			.74
Expresses anger by damaging others' property			.72
In trouble at home			.72
Destroys toys/property of others			.72
Excessive uncontrolled verbal anger			.71
Lies			.70
Behavioral difficulties (past/present)			.69
Temper tantrums			.68
Withdraws from peers/group			.67
Extreme mood swings			.67
Expresses anger by hurting others			.66
Unacceptable showing off			.61
Physically violent			.58
Cruel to other children			.57
Easily led by peers			.57
Disobeys			.55
Shows off for peers			.54
Destroys own toys (ages 3-6)			.51

Reduction in Firesetter Types and Categories of Race

As stated in Chapter 2, Fineman (1995) offers seven commonly identified types of firesetters: curiosity, accidental, cry for help, delinquent, severely disturbed, cognitively impaired, and sociocultural firesetters. However, in examining the frequency of each type of firesetter, it became clear that cognitively impaired firesetters and sociocultural firesetters were not found in numbers proportional to the other types of firesetters ($n = 12$). As a result, cognitively impaired firesetters and sociocultural firesetters were not used in this analysis.

Also, limited numbers of Asian-Americans, Mixed-Americans, and Hispanic Americans were identified ($n = 33$). Because of the limited frequency of each of these categories and the risk of sociocultural variants that may serve to distinguish these groups, they were removed from further analyses.

Preliminary Analyses Regarding the Types of Firesetters

Preliminary analyses were performed to examine information on the sample of juvenile firesetters. 654 males and 222 females were analyzed from MCAIN records for the present study. Significant differences were identified between the sex of the firesetter and the identified type of firesetter (chi-square (1) = 216.04). Frequencies for male and female firesetters characterized as accidental firesetters and delinquent firesetters were very similar. However, females were much more likely to be considered severely disturbed or curiosity firesetters while males were more likely to be identified as cry for help firesetters (see Table 17 and Figure 1).

Table 17

Crosstabulation between types of firesetters and sex of firesetters

Type of Firesetter		Sex		Total
		Male	Female	
Curious	Count	153	63	216
	Percent within type of sex	70.8%	29.2%	100%
	Percent within firesetter	23.4%	28.4%	24.7%
	Percent of total	17.5%	7.2%	24.7%
Accidental				
	Count	99	42	141
	Percent within type of sex	70.2%	29.8%	100%
	Percent within firesetter	15.1%	18.9%	16.1%
	Percent of total	11.3%	4.8%	16.1%
Cry for Help				
	Count	153	27	180
	Percent within type of sex	85%	15%	100%
	Percent within firesetter	23.4%	12.2%	20.5%
	Percent of total	17.5%	3.1%	20.5%
Delinquent				
	Count	159	48	207
	Percent within type of sex	76.8%	23.2%	100%
	Percent within firesetter	24.3%	21.6%	23.6%
	Percent of total	18.2%	5.5%	23.6%
Severely Disturbed				
	Count	90	42	132
	Percent within type of sex	68.2%	31.8%	100%
	Percent within firesetter	13.8%	18.9%	15.1%
	Percent of total	10.3%	4.8%	15.1%
Total				
	Count	654	222	876
	Percent within type of sex	74.7%	25.3%	100%
	Percent within firesetter	100%	100%	100%
	Percent of total	74.7%	25.3%	100%

Figure 1

Crosstabulation between types of firesetters and sex of firesetters

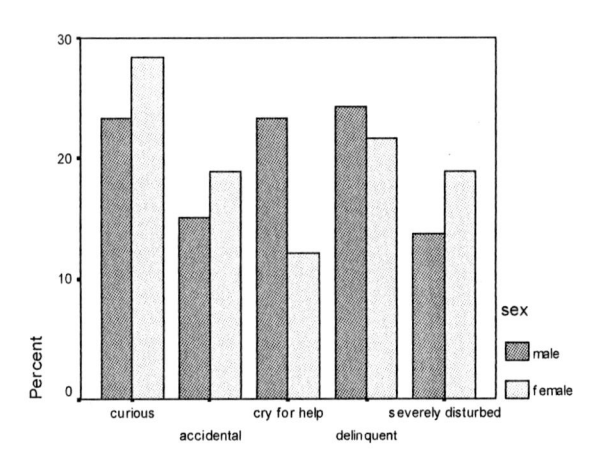

[Bar chart showing percent on y-axis (0-30) and type of firesetter on x-axis (curious, accidental, cry for help, delinquent, severely disturbed), with male and female categories]

type of firesetter

Significant differences also were identified between the age of the firesetter and the identified type of firesetter (chi-square (4) = 32.74). Frequencies for curiosity firesetters were higher in juveniles ages 3 - 6 years of age. Frequencies for accidental firesetters were higher in juveniles ages 7 - 10 years, while frequencies for cry for help firesetters were higher in juveniles 11 – 14 years of age. Delinquent firesetters were most likely to be identified as juveniles ages 15 - 18 years, while severely disturbed firesetters were most likely to be identified as children ages 3 years -6 years of age (see Table 18 and Figure 2).

Table 18

Crosstabulation between types of firesetters and age of firesetters

Type of Firesetter		3-6 years	7-10 years	11-14 years	15-18 years	Total
				Age Groups		
Curious	Count	105	54	30	27	216
	Percent within age	48.6%	25.0%	13.9%	12.5%	100%
	Percent within firesetter	41.7%	17.6%	26.3%	13.2%	24.7%
	Percent of total	12.0%	6.2%	3.4%	3.1%	24.7%
Accidental	Count	30	66	15	30	141
	Percent within age	21.3%	46.8%	10.6%	21.3%	100%
	Percent within firesetter	11.9%	21.6%	13.2%	14.7%	16.1%
	Percent of total	3.4%	7.5%	1.7%	3.4%	16.1%
Cry for Help	Count	48	60	30	42	180
	Percent within age	26.7%	33.3%	16.7%	23.3%	100%
	Percent within firesetter	19.0%	19.6%	26.3%	20.6%	20.5%
	Percent of total	5.5%	6.8%	3.4%	4.8%	20.5%
Delinquent	Count	24	72	27	84	207
	Percent within age	11.6%	34.8%	13.00%	40.6%	100%
	Percent within firesetter	9.5%	23.5%	23.7%	41.2%	23.6%
	Percent of total	2.7%	8.2%	3.1%	9.6%	23.6%
Severely Disturbed	Count	45	54	12	21	132
	Percent within age	34.1%	40.9%	9.1%	15.9%	100%
	Percent within firesetter	17.9%	17.6%	10.5%	10.3%	15.1%
	Percent of total	5.1%	6.2%	1.4%	2.4%	15.1%
Total	Count	252	306	114	204	876
	Percent within type of age	28.8%	34.9%	13.00%	23.3%	100%
	Percent within age group	100%	100%	100%	100%	100%
	Percent of total	28.8%	34.9%	13.00%	23.3%	100%

Figure 2

Crosstabulation between types of firesetters and age of firesetters

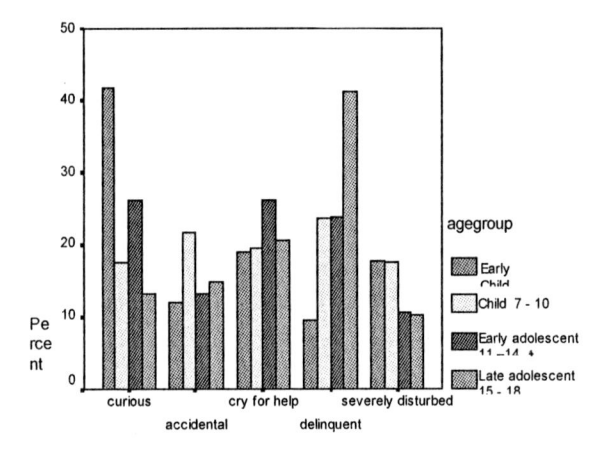

Crosstabulations also confirmed that 495 Caucasian-Americans and 336 African-Americans were sampled from MCAIN records for the present study. The author chose to examine differences between races because of potential biases present in the FEMA documents and MCAIN typing standards. An investigation of the Marion County Arson Tracking System showed that there were insignificant differences with respect to socioeconomic status between Caucasians and African-Americans in the current sample (primarily an inner-city sample of juvenile firesetters). Significant differences were identified between the race of the firesetter and the identified type of firesetter (chi-square (1) = 32.30). Frequencies for Caucasian-American and African-American firesetters characterized as accidental firesetters and delinquent firesetters were very similar. However, Caucasian-American firesetters were much more likely to be considered severely disturbed firesetters or cry for help firesetters when compared with African-American firesetters. African-American firesetters were much more likely to be considered accidental firesetters when compared with Caucasian-American firesetters (see Table 19 and Figure 3).

Table 19

Crosstabulation between types of firesetters and race of firesetters

Type of Firesetter		Race		Total
		Caucasian-American	African-American	
Curious	Count	123	75	198
	Percent within type of race	62.1%	37.9%	100%
	Percent within firesetter	24.8%	22.3%	23.8%
	Percent of total	14.8%	9.0%	23.8%
Accidental				
	Count	63	69	132
	Percent within type of race	47.7%	52.3%	100%
	Percent within firesetter	12.7%	20.5%	15.9%
	Percent of total	7.6%	8.3%	15.9%
Cry for Help				
	Count	117	57	174
	Percent within type of race	67.2%	32.8%	100%
	Percent within firesetter	23.6%	17.0%	20.9%
	Percent of total	14.1%	6.9%	20.9%
Delinquent				
	Count	105	96	201
	Percent within type of race	52.2%	47.8%	100%
	Percent within firesetter	21.2%	28.6%	24.2%
	Percent of total	12.6%	11.6%	24.2%
Severely Disturbed				
	Count	87	39	126
	Percent within type of race	69.0%	31.0%	100%
	Percent within firesetter	17.6%	11.6%	15.2%
	Percent of total	10.5%	4.7%	15.2%
Total				
	Count	495	336	831
	Percent within type of race	59.6%	40.4%	100%
	Percent within firesetter	100%	100%	100%
	Percent of total	59.6%	40.4%	100%

Figure 3

Crosstabulation between types of firesetters and race of firesetters

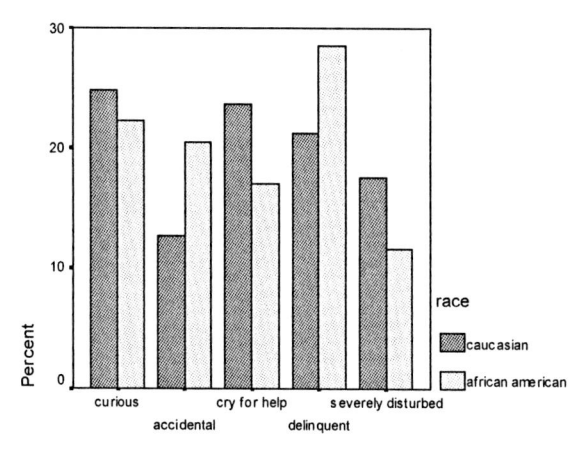

[Bar chart showing percent distribution across firesetter types (curious, accidental, cry for help, delinquent, severely disturbed) by race (caucasian, african american)]

type of firesetter

Enuresis and Recidivistic Firesetting

The first hypothesis tested in this study was that the presence of enuresis and cruelty to animals in juvenile firesetters would be significantly related to recidivistic firesetting. This hypothesis is related to Yarnell's belief in an ego triad among juvenile firesetters, which linked the co-occurrence of enuresis, cruelty to animals and others, and firesetting in youth. For each analysis an a-priori significance level of .01 was chosen.

To determine whether the comorbidity between aspects of the ego triad were significant, the chi-square test was used. No differences were found between groups for firesetting recidivism and the presence of enuresis (chi-square (1) = .16, p = .82). However, juveniles who were identified as being cruel to animals were more likely than children who were not cruel to animals to engage in recidivistic behaviors (chi-square (1) = 25.88, p = .001). When the ego triad (the presence of enuresis and cruelty to animals) was assessed using an analysis of variance (the presence of enuresis and cruelty to animals as relating to recidivistic behaviors), the two-way interaction was not statistically significant (F = 1.69, df = 1, p = .23).

Although cruelty to animals seems to hold integrity as a predictor of recidivistic firesetting behaviors, it is most likely a result of being an externalizing behavior that correlates highly with delinquency. It is interesting to note that the preponderance of enuretic firesetters was significantly higher than in a normative sample of juveniles (t = 6.41, p = .02) (Health Examination Survey Cycle III, 1978). Though firesetting may not be an indicator of recidivism, it would appear to be an effective marker of the bizarre behaviors that are comorbid with firesetting in juveniles.

Predictors of Magnitude of Fire Damages

The second hypothesis tested in this study was that levels of pathology, social skills, and delinquency, as well as the age of the firesetter would predict the magnitude of fire damage from juvenile-set fires. The author hypothesized that the magnitude of the fire damage, as evidenced by the dollar loss related to the fire, also could be explained by the age group of the participant as well as the type of firesetter engaging in recidivistic behaviors.

What variables can be used to identify/predict the magnitude of fire damage from fires set by juvenile girls and boys? Since the best prediction equation is not necessarily the most meaningful equation, the author chose to include explanatory variables that would theoretically explain the magnitude of fire damage. It is believed that high levels of delinquency and social skills would predict the majority of the variance involved in a model meant to predict the magnitude of fire damage.

Regression Analysis. The following variables were included in the model to identify the unique contribution of each variable:

1. *Age.* Although subjects were grouped into age groups for an earlier comparison, juveniles' age in years, drawn from the FEMA Family Fire Risk Questionnaire (Fineman, 1997a) was maintained as a continuous variable for regression analyses.

2. *Type of firesetter.* Five categories of juvenile firesetter classifications were drawn from MCAIN coordinator notes (Spurlin, 1999). Curiosity type, accidental type, cry for help type, delinquency type, and the severely disturbed type were dummy coded (1 = presence of that type, 2 = absence of that type) for inclusion in the regression analysis.

3. *Parent fire risk factor scores.* Each of the resultant factor scores for each individual (pathology, delinquency, and social skills) generated from the exploratory factor analysis of the Parent Fire Risk Questionnaire (Fineman, 1997c) was standardized ($x = 50$; $sd = 10$) for inclusion in the regression analysis.

4. *Magnitude of fire damage.* The variable, magnitude of fire damage, was taken from MCAIN Fire Site Evaluation (Spurlin, 1999). The magnitude of fire damage was estimated at the site of the fire by fire investigators using established industry and insurance protocols. Standards were used to assess the level of financial loss due to the fire.

Statistical significance was established at a predetermined level of .01. The author examined each of the variables that were used, in order to test for assumptions of the multiple regression model.

Error Variance. Based on the observed residual scatterplots, error variance was limited for all values of the explanatory variables. Error variance would enter bias in the model because it will increase relationships found in residuals.

Normality. Based on observed means, standard deviations, skewness, and levels of kurtosis, each of the variables and all linear combinations of the variables were found to approximate normality.

Homoscedasticity/Homogeneity of Variance. Levels of kurtosis were within normal range for measures of age group, gender, pathology, social skills, and delinquency.

Linearity. Linearity was identified by examining types of firesetters against the explaining variables. Based on the residual scatterplots and an examination of the correlations between explanatory variables, there were no problems identified with multicolinearity. In examining the regression plots, linear relationships were evidenced for all predictor and explanatory variables. No outliers were identified in examining the residual scatterplots. The author also examined inter-correlations between both the outcome and explained variables. Correlations between the independent variables were not shown to be above .43, within the normal range for correlations for explaining variables (.60).

Results for the Linear Regression

The multiple regression model was significant, with an R-squared value of .10 ($F_{(9, 887)} = 19.96$, $p = .0001$). The model was able to explain 10% of the variance in the MCAIN coordinator's ratings of the magnitude of fire damage (see Table 20).

Table 20

Coefficients Entered in Regression Model to Predict the Magnitude of Fire Damage by Juveniles

Model	Beta	t-value	Probability
Curiosity firesetter	.24	3.48	.000***
Accidental firesetter	.20	5.34	.000***
Delinquency	-.19	-5.05	.000***
Age	-.16	-4.75	.000***
Severely disturbed firesetter	-.09	-2.28	.01**
Social skills	-.05	-1.54	.12
Pathology	.05	1.57	.12
Delinquent firesetter	-.02	-.56	.58
Cry for help firesetter	-.01	-.53	.67

*** Significant at 0.001 level; ** Significant at 0.01 level

The model identified suggests that the magnitude of loss caused by a juvenile firesetter is best predicted by the type of firesetter involved. If a child is a curiosity firesetter or an accidental firesetter, then the resultant fire is likely to cause greater financial damage. Further, the lower the delinquency of juvenile firesetters, the greater the destructiveness of their fires. The age of the firesetter also appears to be of importance in predicting the magnitude of financial loss caused by a fire, with greater loss being predicted by younger firesetters. Severely disturbed juvenile firesetters were not as likely to cause the magnitude of damage that other firesetters would through fire.

Cross Validation

A cross validation was performed to estimate the stability of the model. Ideally, cross validation would be conducted using two separate samples, but for the present study the sample was split into two halved samples. The difference between R-squared for the halved samples is .03 (R-squared = .12-.09 = .03). The shrinkage identified (.03) is within acceptable limits (.10).

Based on the model used in this multiple regression, age, the type of the firesetter (the presence of curiosity or the absence of delinquent or severely disturbed tendencies), and the absence of delinquency can explain 10% of the variance in the magnitude of fire damage by children and adolescents. The model identified is a stable one. The curiosity of the firesetter was shown to be the strongest predictor of the magnitude of fire damage.

Predictors of Recidivism

The third hypothesis examined in the present study was that recidivism would be predicted by levels of pathology, social skills, and delinquency. The author hypothesized that presence of recidivism could be explained by the age of the participant as well as the type of firesetter engaging in recidivistic behaviors. It was believed that higher levels of delinquency and pathology would predict the majority of the variance involved in a model to predict recidivistic juvenile firesetting.

Regression Analysis. The following variables were included in the model to identify the unique contribution of each variable: (1) age, (2) type of firesetter, (3) pathology, (4) social skills, and (5) delinquency. Predictor variables were the same as those previously used in earlier regression analyses. Recidivistic behavior was the outcome variable, which was identified from information taken from MCAIN files (Spurlin, 1999) and FEMA's Juvenile Firesetter Risk Interview Form (Fineman, 1997b). This measure was a forced-choice item that confirmed whether the firesetter had engaged in recidivistic behaviors following the known firesetting event.

Statistical significance was established at a predetermined level of .01. The author examined each of the variables that were used, in order to test for assumptions of the model. No assumptions were thought to be neglected in performing the linear regression.

Results for the Linear Regression

The multiple regression model was significant, with an R-squared value of .34 (F (9, 887) = 92.43, p = .0001). The model was able to explain 34% of the variance in the MCAIN coordinator's ratings of the recidivistic behaviors of juvenile firesetters (see Table 21).

Table 21

Coefficients Entered in Regression Model to Predict Recidivistic Juvenile Firesetting

Model	Beta	t-value	Probability
Social skills	.27	9.97	.000***
Curiosity firesetter	-.27	-9.47	.000***
Accidental firesetter	-.26	-8.64	.000***
Pathology	.16	5.37	.000***
Delinquency	.15	5.23	.000***
Age	-.09	-3.15	.002**
Cry for help type	-.08	-2.36	.020
Severely disturbed firesetter	.06	1.58	.114
Delinquent type	-.01	-.39	.690

*** Significant at 0.001 level; ** Significant at 0.01 level

Recidivistic behaviors can be predicted by high levels of social skills, the absence of curious or accidental characteristics, and higher levels of pathology or delinquency.

Cross Validation

A cross validation was performed to estimate the stability of the model. Ideally, cross validation would be conducted using two separate samples, but for the present study the sample was split into two halved samples. The difference between R-squared for the halved samples is .005 (R-squared = .345 - .34 = .005). The shrinkage identified (.005) is within acceptable limits (.10).

Based on the model used in this multiple regression, social skills, delinquency, and pathology, in addition to the absence of curious or accidental firesetting characteristics can explain 34% of the variance in the recidivistic firesetting of children and adolescents. The model identified is a stable one. The measure of social skills of the firesetter was shown to be the strongest predictor of recidivism.

Predictors of the Typology of the Juvenile Firesetter

The fourth hypothesis examined in the present study was that the typology of the juvenile firesetter would be predicted by both levels of pathology, social skills, and delinquency, as well as the age of the firesetter. The author hypothesized that types of firesetting also could be explained by the gender and the race of the participant. It is believed that higher levels of pathology and delinquency would predict most types of firesetting. For each of the five types of juvenile firesetters identified, a separate regression analysis was performed.

The following variables were included in the study to identify the unique contribution of each variable to each typology: (1) age, (2) gender (3) race, (4) pathology, (5) social skills, and (6) delinquency. Type of firesetter was specified in the MCAIN files (Spurlin, 1999). Statistical significance was established at a predetermined level of .01.

Results for the Linear Regression: Curiosity Firesetters

The multiple regression model was significant, with an R-squared value of .10 ($F(6, 842) = 25.13$, $p = .0001$). The model was able to explain 10% of the variance in the MCAIN coordinator's ratings of firesetters as curiosity firesetters (see Table 22).

Table 22

Coefficients Entered in Regression Model to Predict Curiosity Firesetters

Model	Beta	t-value	Probability
Social skills	-.19	-5.71	.000***
Age	-.17	-5.20	.000***
Pathology	-.15	-4.61	.000***
Delinquency	-.15	-4.41	.000***
Race	.06	1.93	.050
Sex	-.02	1.21	.230

*** Significant at 0.001 level; ** Significant at 0.01 level

Curiosity firesetters can be explained as younger juveniles with low levels of delinquency and low levels of pathology. Curiosity firesetters also can be explained as juveniles who have few problems socializing or expressing emotions.

Cross Validation

A cross validation was performed to estimate the stability of the model. Ideally, cross validation would be conducted using two separate samples, but for the present study the sample was split into two halved samples. The difference between R-squared for the halved samples is .01 (R-squared = .11-.10 = .01). The shrinkage identified (.01) is within acceptable limits (.10).

Based on the model used in this multiple regression, age, low levels of pathology, low levels of social skills, and low levels of delinquency can explain 10% of the variance in predicting that juvenile firesetters are curiosity firesetters. The model identified is a stable one.

The level of social skills was shown to be the strongest predictor of types of firesetting.

Results for the Linear Regression: Accidental Firesetters

The multiple regression model was significant, with an R-squared value of .08 (F (6, 842) = 19.27, p = .0001). The model was able to explain 8% of the variance in the MCAIN coordinator's ratings of firesetters as accidental firesetters (see Table 23).

Table 23

Coefficients Entered in Regression Model to Predict Accidental Firesetters

Model	Beta	t-value	Probability
Social skills	-.21	-6.22	.000***
Pathology	-.15	-4.37	.000***
Delinquency	-.10	-3.12	.000***
Race	-.08	-2.35	.02
Age	-.04	-1.12	.26
Sex	-.04	-1.07	.29

*** Significant at 0.001 level; ** Significant at 0.01 level

Accidental firesetters can be explained as juveniles with low levels of delinquency and low levels of pathology. Accidental firesetters also can be explained as juveniles who have few problems socializing or expressing emotions.

Cross Validation

A cross validation was performed to estimate the stability of the model. Ideally, cross validation would be conducted using two separate samples, but for the present study the sample was split into two halved samples. The difference between R-squared for the halved samples is .02 (R-squared = .10 - .08 = .02). The shrinkage identified (.02) is within acceptable limits (.10).

Based on the model used in this multiple regression, low levels of pathology, low levels of social skills, and low levels of delinquency can explain 10% of the variance in predicting that juvenile firesetters are accidental firesetters. The model identified is a stable one. The level of social skills was shown to be the strongest predictor of accidental types of firesetting.

Results for the Linear Regression: Cry for Help Firesetters

The multiple regression model was significant, with an R-squared value of .07 ($F_{(6, 842)}$ = 17.66, p = .0001). The model was able to explain 8% of the variance in the MCAIN coordinator's ratings of firesetters as cry for help firesetters (see Table 24).

Table 24

Coefficients Entered in Regression Model to Predict Cry for Help Firesetters

Model	Beta	t-value	Probability
Social skills	-.18	-5.21	.000***
Pathology	-.16	-4.79	.000***
Sex	.10	3.09	.002**
Race	.03	1.99	.04
Age	.03	.89	.38
Delinquency	.02	.69	.49

*** Significant at 0.001 level; ** Significant at 0.01 level

Cry for help firesetters can be explained as juveniles who have problems socializing or expressing emotions. Cry for help firesetters also can be explained as juveniles with low levels of pathology. Cry for help firesetters also are more likely to be female than male firesetters.

Cross Validation

A cross validation was performed to estimate the stability of the model. Ideally, cross validation would be conducted using two separate samples, but for the present study the sample was split into two halved samples. The difference between R-squared for the halved samples is .01 (R-squared = .08-.07 = .01). The shrinkage identified (.01) is within acceptable limits (.10).

Based on the model used in this multiple regression, low levels of pathology, low levels of social skills, and gender can predict 8% of the variance in predicting that juvenile firesetters are cry for help firesetters. The model identified is a stable one. The low levels of social skills was shown to be the strongest predictor of the cry for help type of firesetter.

Results for the Linear Regression: Delinquent Firesetters

The multiple regression model was significant, with an R-squared value of .22 (F (10, 842) = 55.83, p = .0001). The model was able to explain 22% of the variance in the MCAIN coordinator's ratings of firesetters as delinquent firesetters (see Table 25).

Table 25

Coefficients Entered in Regression Model to Predict Delinquent Firesetters

Model	Beta	t-value	Probability
Pathology	-.23	-7.43	.000***
Age	.22	6.87	.000***
Delinquency	.20	6.60	.000***
Social skills	-.19	-6.03	.000***
Race	-.13	-4.08	.002
Sex	.01	.26	.79

*** Significant at 0.001 level; ** Significant at 0.01 level

Delinquent firesetters can be explained as older juveniles with low levels of pathology and high levels of delinquency. Delinquent firesetters also can be explained as juveniles who have few problems socializing or expressing emotions.

Cross Validation

A cross validation was performed to estimate the stability of the model. Ideally, cross validation would be conducted using two separate samples, but for the present study the sample was split into two halved samples. The difference between R-squared for the halved samples is .03 (R-squared = .24-.21 = .03). The shrinkage identified (.03) is within acceptable limits (.10).

Based on the model used in this multiple regression, age, low levels of pathology, low levels of social skills, and high levels of delinquency can explain 22% of the variance in predicting that juvenile firesetters are delinquent firesetters. The model identified is a stable one. Low levels of pathology were shown to be the strongest predictor of delinquent types of firesetting. Race and gender were not significant predictors of delinquent types of firesetting.

Results for the Linear Regression: Severely Disturbed Firesetters

The multiple regression model was significant, with an R-squared value of .37 ($F_{(6, 842)} = 162.42$, $p = .0001$). The model was able to explain 37% of the variance in the MCAIN coordinator's ratings of fireseters as severely disturbed firesetters (see Table 26).

Table 26

Coefficients Entered in Regression Model to Predict Severely Disturbed Firesetters

Model	Beta	t-value	Probability
Delinquency	-.56	-20.34	.000***
Pathology	.25	8.85	.000***
Race	.06	2.29	.002**
Age	.05	1.89	.060
Sex	-.05	-1.74	.080
Social skills	.02	.98	.330

*** Significant at 0.001 level; ** Significant at 0.01 level

Severely disturbed firesetters can be explained as juveniles with low levels of delinquency and high levels of pathology. Severely disturbed firesetters also are more likely to be Caucasian-American than African-American.

Cross Validation

A cross validation was performed to estimate the stability of the model. Ideally, cross validation would be conducted using two separate samples, but for the present study the sample was split into two halved samples. The difference between R-squared for the halved samples is .02 (R-squared = .38-.35 = .03). The shrinkage identified (.03) is within acceptable limits (.10).

Based on the model used in this multiple regression, race, low levels of delinquency, and high levels of pathology can explain 37% of the variance in predicting that juvenile firesetters are severely disturbed firesetters. The model identified is a stable one. Low levels of delinquency were shown to be the strongest predictor of severely disturbed types of firesetting.

Developmental Trends in Juvenile Firesetting

The fifth hypothesis examined in the present study was that a developmental pattern would be identified in examining factors related to juvenile firesetting. A between-subjects analysis of variance was performed for each of the factors identified in the exploratory analyses (pathology, social skills, delinquency) as being related to firesetting in juveniles. For each analysis an a-priori significance level of .01 was chosen.

Pathology. The major analysis concerned a 2 x 2 x 4 x 5 between-subjects factorial ANOVA using the total number of individual responses made on the pathology factor as the dependent measure, with race, sex, age groups, and type of firesetter as independent variables. 831 participants were analyzed for the between-subjects analyses of variance. Since results for this study were exploratory, only main effects and interactions between two predictors were examined.

The between-subjects analysis of variance confirmed that developmental trends were evidenced in examining pathology within juvenile firesetters ($F_{(1, 830)} = 8.72$, $p = .0001$). Main effects for age groups (from early childhood to late adolescence) were significant ($F_{(3, 830)} = 4.53$, $p = .004$). A Bonferroni post-hoc technique indicated that significant differences at the .01 level were found between all permutations of the age levels (child = 50.63, child $M = 48.19$, early adolescent $M = 49.05$, late adolescent $M = 51.04$), except for children and early adolescents, which neared significance at the .06 level. However, no significant main effects were evidenced based on sex (females $M = 50.36$, males $M = 49.21$) ($F_{(1, 830)} = .353$, $p = .53$) nor on race (Caucasian-American $M = 50.03$, African-American $M = 49.29$), although differences with respect to race neared significance ($F_{(1, 830)} = 5.95$, $p = .015$).

One of the strongest results identified with respect to pathology was identified when examining differences between the types of firesetters ($F (4, 830) = 17.98, p = .0001$). A Bonferroni post-hoc technique indicated that significant differences at the .01 level were found between all permutations of the nonpathological types of firesetters (curiosity type $M = 46.32$, accidental type $M = 46.81$, cry for help type $M = 47.04$) and the pathological types (delinquent type $M = 54.05$, severely disturbed type $M = 54.49$). However, no differences between the subtypes in the pathological and nonpathological groupings were identified.

Significant interactions were identified between age groups and sex ($F (3, 830) = 10.97$, $p = .001$) in female children ages 3 - 6 years showing higher levels of pathology. Significant interactions also were identified between age group and type of firesetter ($F (12, 830) = 2.99$, $p = .0001$), with the highest levels of pathology found in children ages 3 - 10 identified as severely disturbed. No significant interaction was identified between age group and race ($F (3, 830) = 1.28, p = .28$). Nearly significant interactions were identified between type of firesetter and sex ($F (5, 830) = 2.43, p = .046$). However, significant interactions were identified between type of firesetter and race ($F (4, 830) = 12.58, p = .0001$), with Caucasian-American severely disturbed firesetters showing the highest levels of pathology. R-squared verified that this model accounted for 41% of the variance (see Table 27).

Table 27

Analysis of variance symmetry of pathology in juvenile firesetters by sex, race, age group, and type of firesetter

Source	SS	df	MS	F	p
Sex (A)	21.16	1	21.16	.35	.550
Race (B)	357.50	1	357.50	5.96	.020
Age Group (C)	816.46	3	816.46	4.53	.000***
Type Firesetter (D)	4317.99	4	4317.99	17.98	.000***
Age x Sex	1976.80	3	658.93	10.98	.041
Age x Race	230.35	3	76.78	1.28	.280
Age x Type	2151.17	12	179.26	2.99	.000***
Type x Sex	583.28	4	145.82	2.43	.046
Type x Race	3020.26	4	755.06	12.58	.000***
Error	46103.77	768	60.03		
Total	2131112.00	830			

*** Significant at 0.001 level; ** Significant at 0.01 level

Social skills. The major analysis for social skills concerned a 2 x 2 x 4 x 5 between-subjects factorial ANOVA using the total number of individual responses made on the social skills factor as the dependent measure, with race, sex, age groups, and type of firesetter as independent variables. 831 participants were analyzed for the between-subjects analyses of variance. Since results for this study were exploratory, only main effects and interactions between two predictors were examined.

The between-subjects analysis of variance confirmed that developmental trends were evidenced in examining social skills within juvenile firesetters ($F (1, 830) = 5.92$, $p = .0001$). Main effects for age groups (from early childhood to late adolescence) were significant

(F (3, 830) = 6.52, p = .0001). A Bonferroni post-hoc technique indicated that significant differences at the .01 level were found between all permutations of the age levels (child M = 50.39, child M = 51.35, early adolescent M = 53.90, late adolescent M = 56.67). Significant main effects were not evidenced for sex (F (1, 830) = 1.124, p = .29) nor for race (F (1, 830) = 5.95, p = .056).

One of the strongest results identified with respect to social skills was identified when examining differences between the types of firesetters (F (4, 830) = 15.44, p = .0001). A Bonferroni post-hoc technique indicated that significant differences at the .01 level were found between permutations of the nonpathological types of firesetters (curiosity type M = 46.72, accidental type M = 44.41) and other types of firesetters (cry for help type M = 52.27, delinquent type M = 53.14, severely disturbed type M = 50.97).

Significant interactions also were identified between age groups and sex (F (3, 830) = 4.28, p = .005), with early adolescent males showing more problems with social skills than other permutations. Significant interactions were identified between the age group and type of firesetter (F (12, 830) = 3.67, p = .0001), with the highest levels of social skills being found in juveniles ages 15 - 18 years identified as delinquent types. Unlike with the pathology factor, a significant interaction was identified between age group and race (F (3, 830) = 12.54, p = .001), with African-American early adolescents scoring highest in social skills. A significant interaction also was identified between type of firesetter and sex (F (4, 830) = 4.72, p = .001), with male cry for help firesetters showing the greatest preponderance of social skills. Finally, significant interactions were identified between type of firesetter and race (F (4, 830) = 6.45, p = .0001), with social skills being highest in African-American delinquent types. R-squared verified that this model accounted for 33% of the theorized variance (see Table 28).

Table 28

Analysis of variance symmetry of social skills in juvenile firesetters by sex, race, age group, and type of firesetter

Source	SS	df	MS	F	p
Sex (A)	81.29	1	81.29	1.12	.289
Race (B)	264.18	1	264.18	3.65	.056
Age Group (C)	1413.93	3	471.31	6.52	.000***
Type Firesetter (D)	4466.47	4	1116.62	15.44	.000***
Age x Sex	928.07	3	309.36	4.28	.005**
Age x Race	1864.94	3	466.24	6.45	.000***
Age x Type	3186.00	12	265.50	3.67	.000***
Type x Sex	1366.77	4	341.69	4.72	.001**
Type x Race	1864.94	4	466.24	6.45	.000***
Error	55555.86	768	72.34		
Total	2151822.00	830			

*** Significant at 0.001 level; ** Significant at 0.01 level

Delinquency. The major analysis for delinquency concerned a 2 x 2 x 4 x 5 between-subjects factorial ANOVA using the total number of individual responses made on the delinquency factor as the dependent measure, with race, sex, age groups, and type of firesetter as independent variables. 831 participants were analyzed for the between-subjects analyses of variance. Since results for this study were exploratory, only main effects and interactions between two predictors were examined.

The between-subjects analysis of variance confirmed that developmental trends were evidenced in examining delinquency within juvenile firesetters ($F_{(1, 830)} = 11.42$, $p = .0001$).

However, main effects for age groups (from early childhood to late adolescence) were not significant ($F(3, 830) = 1.58$, $p = .19$). No significant main effects were evidenced based for sex ($F(1, 830) = .002$, $p = .96$) nor on race ($F(1, 830) = 2.08$, $p = .15$).

One of the strongest results identified with respect to delinquency was identified when examining differences between the types of firesetters ($F(4, 830) = 67.00$, $p = .0001$). A Bonferroni post-hoc technique indicated that significant differences at the .01 level were found between all permutations of the nonpathological types of firesetters (curiosity type $M = 18.87$, accidental type $M = 17.93$, cry for help type $M = 18.34$) and the pathological types (delinquent type $M = 24.08$, severely disturbed type $M = 25.04$). However, no differences were identified between the pathological and nonpathological subgroups.

No significant interaction was identified between age groups and sex ($F(3, 830) = 1.15$, $p = .33$). However, a significant interaction was identified between age group and type of firesetter ($F(12, 830) = 2.06$, $p = .01$), with juveniles ages 11 - 14 years who are identified as delinquent types showing the greatest levels of delinquency. A significant interaction also was identified between age group and race ($F(3, 830) = 4.42$, $p = .004$), with African-American adolescents ages 15 - 18 years showing the highest levels of delinquency. Significant interactions were identified between type of firesetter and sex ($F(4, 830) = 5.56$, $p = .0001$), with delinquent type males identified as having the highest levels of delinquency. Interactions between type of firesetter and race ($F(4, 830) = 4.94$, $p = .001$) also were significant, with African-American delinquent types showing the highest levels of delinquency. R-squared verified that this model accounted for 48% of the theorized variance (see Table 29).

Table 29

Analysis of variance symmetry of delinquency in juvenile firesetters by sex, race, age group, and type of firesetter

Source	SS	df	MS	F	p
Sex (A)	.100	1	.100	.02	.966
Race (B)	117.69	1	117.69	2.08	.149
Age Group (C)	266.96	3	88.99	1.58	.194
Type Firesetter (D)	15135.55	4	3783.89	67.06	.000***
Age x Sex	194.99	3	64.99	1.15	.328
Age x Race	748.51	3	249.50	4.42	.001**
Age x Type	1391.25	12	115.94	2.06	.01
Type x Sex	1256.57	4	314.14	5.56	.000***
Type x Race	1117.51	4	279.38	4.95	.001**
Error	43369.78	768	56.47		
Total	2167912.00	830			

*** Significant at 0.001 level; ** Significant at 0.01 level

CHAPTER SIX
DISCUSSION

This study accomplished two primary purposes. First, this study assessed the psychometric properties of the Federal Emergency Management Agency (FEMA) questionnaires used to record juvenile firesetting events (Fineman, 1997a, 1997b, 1997c). Second, this study initiated preliminary analyses that (1) contributed to the identification of a typology of firesetters, (2) accounted for variance in the severity of fires set by juveniles, and (3) predicted the likelihood of recidivistic behaviors in juvenile firesetters.

Psychometric Properties of the FEMA Forms (Fineman, 1997a, 1997b, 1997c)

Though the Family Fire Risk Inventory (Fineman, 1997a) and the Juvenile Fire Risk Inventory (Fineman, 1997b) both evidenced low reliability, as well as limited ability to identify recidivistic firesetters or psychological problems with them, the Parent Fire Risk Questionnaire (Fineman, 1997c) appears adequate for both purposes. Given the data in this study, it would be appropriate for the Federal Emergency Management Agency to reexamine its dependence on the Family Fire Risk Inventory (Fineman, 1997a) and the Juvenile Fire Risk Inventory (Fineman, 1997b). The psychometric assessment of the Family Fire Risk Inventory (Fineman, 1997a) and Juvenile Fire Risk Inventory (Fineman, 1997b) suggests a need for substantial revision.

Further, the factors derived from the Parent Fire Risk Inventory appear to differentiate well among the types of firesetters, although limited insight into curiosity firesetters was found. It may be that characteristics that are predictive of curiosity firesetters are not presently found on these forms. Further investigation of characteristics that may predict curiosity firesetters is needed.

Enuresis and Recidivistic Firesetting

The first hypothesis tested in this study was that the presence of enuresis and cruelty to animals in juvenile firesetters would be significantly related to recidivistic firesetting. This hypothesis was related to Yarnell's belief in an ego triad among juvenile firesetters, which linked the co-occurrence of enuresis, cruelty to animals and others, and firesetting in youth. No differences were found between groups for firesetting recidivism and the presence of enuresis. However, juveniles who were identified as being cruel to animals were more likely than children who were not cruel to animals to engage in recidivistic behaviors. Further, when compared with a sizable sample of juveniles, the incidence of enuresis was elevated in the present sample.

It is not surprising that firesetting, bedwetting, and cruelty to animals were identified simultaneously in juveniles; the studies that validated the triad were performed using institutionalized samples. Those reports were based on case study reviews and data extrapolated from projective instruments (Kaufman et al., 1961; Lester, 1975; Macht & Mack, 1968; Quinsey, Chaplin, & Upfold, 1989; Rothstein, 1963). Although cruelty to animals seems to hold some integrity as a predictor of recidivistic firesetting, it is most likely a result of being a strong externalizing behavior that correlates highly with delinquency.

Juvenile firesetters have been shown to be more likely than other groups of juveniles to be cruel to children or animals (Quinsey, Chaplin, & Upfold, 1989; Sakheim & Osborn, 1999; Sakheim, Osborn, & Abrams, 1991; Saunders & Awad, 1991). However, the predictiveness of this factor is limited (Blumberg, 1981; Heath, Gayton, & Hardesty, 1976; Showers & Pickrell, 1987). Justice, Justice, and Kraft (1974) also questioned whether the ego triad is an adequate system of identification in predicting violent behavior in adulthood. The authors assert that the ego triad is largely identified as occurring simultaneously with factors that may be better predictors of violent adult behaviors.

However, it is interesting to note that the preponderance of enuretic firesetters was significantly higher than in a normative sample of juveniles. Though bedwetting may not be an indicator of recidivism, it would appear to be an effective marker of the bizarre behaviors that are comorbid with firesetting in juveniles. It is interesting to find such a significant difference in enuretic behaviors between a normative population and the present study's sample. Though Freud (1932) and Yarnell (1940) appear to be limited and outdated theoretical approaches, the relationship between juvenile firesetting and enuresis continues as does cruelty to animals.

Predictors of Magnitude of Fire Damage

The second hypothesis tested in this study was that levels of pathology, social skills, and delinquency, as well as the age of the firesetter would predict the magnitude of juvenile-set fire damage. The author hypothesized that magnitude of the fire damage, as evidenced by the dollar loss related to the fire, also could be explained by the age group of the participant as well as the type of firesetter engaging in recidivistic behaviors.

The multiple regression model was significant, and was able to explain 10% of the variance in the MCAIN coordinator's ratings of the magnitude of fire damage based on the model used. The limited variance that could be explained may be due to the skewed nature of the dependent variable, or perhaps is due to the limited predictive nature of psychological variables in estimating a dollar loss.

The model identified suggests that the magnitude of loss caused by a juvenile firesetter is best predicted by the type of firesetter involved. If a child is a curiosity firesetter or an accidental firesetter, then the resultant fire is likely to cause greater financial damage. The age of the firesetter also appears to be of importance in predicting the magnitude of financial loss caused by a fire, with greater loss being predicted by younger firesetters.

Further, it also was discovered that the lower the delinquency of juvenile firesetters, the greater the destructiveness of their fires. Severely disturbed juvenile firesetters were not as likely as other firesetters to cause the magnitude of damage that other firesetters would through fire. The curiosity of the firesetter was shown to be the strongest predictor of the magnitude of the fire.

The highest damage caused by juvenile firesetters occurred in fires set by young children for curious reasons or accidentally. The experimentation that these children engage in is often more destructive than other combinations of firesetters and settings because young firesetters often set fire to paper or objects in their bedrooms. The damage caused by the flame is often not discovered by caretakers until the child notifies them (which often does not occur for some time) (Kolko & Kazdin, 1998). Though these curiosity or young firesetters often show remorse for their behaviors following the incident, they tend not to understand the severity of their behaviors until after the damage is done.

It is thought that most children are inherently curious about fire. However, curiosity firesetters are likely to have early involvement with firesetting, and are generally more interested in fire than other types of juvenile firesetters (Kolko & Kazdin, 1991). Because of the dangerousness surrounding younger and curiosity firesetters, parents and caregivers need to educate their youth about the responsible adult uses of fire. Many fire professionals believe that educating youth about fire safety and the dangers of firesetting can reduce the recidivism rate among juvenile firesetters (Federal Emergency Management Agency, 1996). Also, educational interventions may reduce recidivism rates in early childhood firesetters following the integration of fire safety measures within educational programming, general childcare systems, or family welfare schemes (Adler et al., 1994; Eisler, 1972).

It may be, however, that estimated cost of fire damage set by juvenile firesetters may not be a very useful dependent variable as a result of the skewed nature of the variable.

Predictors of Recidivism

The third hypothesis examined in the present study was that recidivism would be predicted by levels of pathology, social skills, and delinquency. The author hypothesized that presence of recidivism could be explained by the age of the participant as well as the type of firesetter engaging in recidivistic behaviors. It was believed that higher levels of delinquency and pathology would predict the majority of the variance involved in a model meant to predict recidivistic juvenile firesetting. This study found that recidivistic behaviors can be predicted by high levels of social skills, the absence of curious or accidental characteristics, and higher levels of pathology or delinquency.

The multiple regression model was significant, and was able to explain 34% of the variance in the MCAIN coordinator's ratings of the recidivistic behaviors of juvenile firesetters based on the model used. Firesetting research has neglected the connections between juvenile recidivism and patterns of delinquency. Similar to results identified by Heaven (1994), this study found that adolescents that were self-described as delinquent were more likely to engage in recidivistic, violent behaviors.

As with Kolko and Kazdin (1991, 1994), this study found that recidivistic juvenile firesetters report higher levels of limited social skills, higher levels of delinquency, and are more likely to connect their deviance with covert aggressive expressions when compared with other firesetters. Based on the model used in this multiple regression, delinquency, pathology, and social skills, in addition to the absence of curious or accidental firesetting characteristics can explain 34% of the variance in the recidivistic firesetting of children and adolescents. The measure of social skills of the firesetter was shown to be the strongest predictor of recidivism.

Predictors of the Typology of the Juvenile Firesetter

The fourth hypothesis examined in the present study was that the typology of the juvenile firesetter would be predicted by both levels of pathology, social skills, and delinquency, as well as the age of the firesetter. The author hypothesized that types of firesetting also could be explained by the gender and the race of the participant. It was believed that higher levels of pathology and delinquency would predict most types of firesetting.

Curiosity firesetter. The multiple regression model for curiosity firesetters was significant, and was able to explain 10% of the variance in the MCAIN coordinator's ratings of firesetters as curiosity firesetters. Curiosity firesetters can be explained as younger juveniles with low levels of delinquency and low levels of pathology. Curiosity firesetters also can be explained as juveniles who have few problems socializing or expressing emotions.

This study confirmed that most curious firesetters are young children (juveniles ages 3 to 6 years) who engage in firesetting as experimentation. Curiosity firesetters were likely to have early involvement with firesetting, and were generally more interested in fire than other types of juvenile firesetters, leading to greater damage and destructiveness (also see Kolko & Kazdin, 1991).

Based on the model used in this multiple regression, age, low levels of pathology, low levels of social skills, and low levels of delinquency can explain 10% of the variance in predicting that juvenile firesetters are curiosity firesetters. The level of social skills was shown to be the strongest predictor of types of firesetting. Race and gender were not significant predictors of curiosity types of firesetting.

Accidental firesetter. The multiple regression model for accidental firesetters was significant, and was able to explain 8% of the variance in the MCAIN coordinator's ratings of firesetters as accidental firesetters based on the model used. Accidental firesetters were identified in this study as juveniles with low levels of delinquency and low levels of pathology. Accidental firesetters also can be explained as juveniles who have few problems socializing or expressing emotions. As with earlier studies accidental firesetters are usually children under the age of 11 years.

Based on the model used in this multiple regression, low levels of pathology, low levels of social skills, and low levels of delinquency can explain 10% of the variance in predicting that juvenile firesetters are curiosity firesetters. The model identified is a stable one. The level of social skills was shown to be the strongest predictor of types of firesetting. Gender was not a significant predictor of accidental types of firesetting.

Cry for help firesetter. The multiple regression model for cry for help firesetters was significant, and was able to explain 8% of the variance in the MCAIN coordinator's ratings of firesetters as curiosity firesetters based on the model used. Cry for help firesetters can be explained as juveniles with low levels of pathology. Cry for help firesetters also can be explained as juveniles who do not have problems socializing or expressing emotions. Cry for help firesetters also are more likely to be female than male firesetters.

It is interesting to note that the only gender difference identified in this study was identified with respect to cry for help firesetters. It was surprising that females, who are socialized to externalize emotions, could be found in situations that warranted the use of covert expressions of emotions, such as with firesetting.

It also is interesting to note that Caucasian-Americans could be more likely than African-Americans to be considered cry for help firesetters. It would appear that African-American youth are at a heightened risk of being labeled deviant or delinquent firesetters than to be labeled in need of emotional support or assistance. Future studies of firesetters may want to examine whether gender or racial biases exist in the communities where firesetters are identified.

Based on the model used in this multiple regression, low levels of pathology, low levels of social skills, race, and gender can predict 8% of the variance in predicting that juvenile firesetters are cry for help firesetters. Low levels of social skills were shown to be the strongest predictor of types of firesetting.

Delinquent firesetter. The multiple regression model was significant, and was able to explain 22% of the variance in the MCAIN coordinator's ratings of firesetters as delinquent firesetters based on the model used. Delinquent firesetters can be explained as older juveniles with low levels of pathology and high levels of delinquency. Delinquent firesetters also can be explained as juveniles who have few problems socializing or expressing emotions.

Delinquent firesetting was found to have a developmental trend. Delinquent tendencies were found to begin during preadolescence and increase throughout adolescence. As with the findings of Harris and Rice (1996), during preadolescence delinquent firesetters show some empathy for others. However, adolescent delinquent firesetters show little empathy for others, or little conscience for their behaviors. As with prior studies the greatest amount of deviancy and behavioral dysfunction was identified with adolescent firesetters (also see Kolko & Kazdin, 1991). Firesetting in this group is more easily extinguished than the other personality and behavior problems that accompany the firesetting (Showers & Pickrell, 1987).

Unlike earlier studies of juvenile firesetters, this study was one of the first to identify that delinquent firesetters are less likely than other types of firesetters to have low levels of pathology. It would appear that some firesetters are driven to engage in firesetting due to an inability to express anger in appropriate manners. Further research needs to be performed which can identify the reasons behind why these firesetters turn to fire to express their feelings, rather than some other form of deviance or vandalism.

Based on the model used in this multiple regression, age, low levels of pathology, low levels of social skills, and high levels of delinquency can explain 22% of the variance in predicting that juvenile firesetters are delinquent firesetters. Low levels of pathology were shown to be the strongest predictor of delinquent types of firesetting. Race and gender were not significant predictors of delinquent types of firesetting.

Severely disturbed firesetter. The multiple regression model for the severely disturbed firesetter was significant, and was able to explain 37% of the variance in the MCAIN coordinator's ratings of firesetters as delinquent firesetters based on the model used. Severely disturbed firesetters can be explained as juveniles with low levels of delinquency and high levels of pathology. As found when looking at the relationship between delinquent firesetters and pathology, an inverse relationship appears to exist between delinquency and severely disturbed firesetters: the lower the level of delinquency in severely disturbed firesetters, the higher the pathology and the disturbed nature of the firesetter.

Severely disturbed firesetters also are more likely to be Caucasian-American than African-American. It is interesting to note that African-Americans were not as likely as Caucasian-Americans to have been identified as severely disturbed firesetters. Perhaps African-American youth are stereotyped as being more delinquent or oppositional, as with other forms of nontraditional behaviors. It is unknown whether other studies have identified similar differences with respect to race.

Unlike the "cry for help" firesetter who tend to show similar symptomatology as a result of environmental circumstances, these children are likely to have early signs as a result of individual psychopathology. Unlike Kolko and Kazdin (1988) severely disturbed firesetters were not shown to have higher levels of recidivism than other types of firesetters. Though social neglect and parental dysfunction are likely to be correlated with firesetters identified as severely disturbed, further research needs to be initiated which answers the question of how parental dysfunction and social neglect contribute to firesetting (also see Heath et al., 1976).

Based on the model used in this multiple regression, race, low levels of delinquency, and high levels of pathology can explain 37% of the variance in predicting that juvenile firesetters are severely disturbed firesetters. Low levels of delinquency were shown to be the strongest predictor of severely disturbed types of firesetting.

Dependent Variables Under Investigation

The community that studies firesetters has differed in the dependent variables used in their investigations. In fact, fire professionals also disagree as to the most effective ways to track juvenile firesetting. The typology of firesetters proved helpful in better understanding the nature of juvenile firesetting behavior. Developmental aspects of these behaviors also proved interesting in better understanding why juveniles of various ages turn to the maladaptive use of fire.

Though recidivism is a characteristic that is critical for people in the fire service to understand, it was not a helpful variable in understanding the nature of firesetting behaviors. The magnitude of fire damage based on dollar loss, though similarly important to people in the fire service, was not helpful in the present study. Recidivism and high dollar loss due to fire appear to occur for reasons other than are found within the individual setting the fire. As such, it would be important to study the environs and external character of a fire site in order to more fully understand how these variables fluctuate from fire to fire and from juvenile firesetter to juvenile firesetter.

Firesetting across Early Childhood and Adolescence

Examination of the differences between age groups can improve professionals' understanding of firesetting. Though a largely unexplored area of study, it is now believed that maladaptive firesetting and the reasons for firesetting differ across early childhood and adolescence as a result of developmental changes.

The results of this study suggest that juvenile firesetting follows an age-related developmental trend, with children (children ages 7 to 10) showing greater levels of firesetting than other age groups. It is interesting to note that differences between age groups were identified when using predictors like pathology and social skills, but not for delinquency. It may be that firesetters as a group may show higher delinquent tendencies from a younger age, and are therefore, not as likely to show differences as they mature (which may be a result of the sample under examination). It also may be an aberration of the data identified for this group, which included a large number of children living in poverty and violence, who may be more likely than other children to mimic the violent and destructive behaviors modeled in their immediate environments.

As identified previously throughout the literature, limited differences exist between males and females on firesetting. The psychodynamic models' claim that boys engage in firesetting due to urethral releases of pent-up anxieties and that girls engage in firesetting to escape to fantasies of containing the power of a phallus clearly are limited after reviewing these results. It may be that girls and boys, when reared in environments with limited structure and poor social dynamics, are more prone to using fire in maladaptive ways.

An interesting result of this study identified racial differences between Caucasians and African-Americans with respect to pathology. Caucasians were found to be higher in measures of pathology at every age group and in every firesetting type, perhaps indicating that African-American firesetters might not reveal as many externalizing characteristics prior to recidivism. Though racial differences were discovered, it is likely that these differences are the result of inherent biases in the MCAIN coding system, rather than actual differences between Caucasians and African-Americans. That differences would be discovered in a sample quite similar in socioeconomic status is disturbing. The elevated level of psychopathology among African-American participants must be viewed with caution. The possibility exists that the instrument and coding system hold biases. Further investigations are warranted with samples that can be better matched on socioeconomic and ethnic factors.

Types of Juvenile Firesetters

Predictors of juvenile firesetting differed for each age-related grouping of firesetter, with delinquent and social skills showing greater strength during early and late adolescence when compared to earlier periods of development. Pathology predicted firesetting fairly equally across juvenile development, but showed significantly higher levels during preadolescence and early adolescence than any other period.

It was interesting that the post-hoc results indicated significant differences between all permutations of the nonpathological types of firesetters (curiosity type, accidental type, and cry for help type) and the pathological types (delinquent type, severely disturbed type), but no differences between these subgroups were identified. It also is interesting that the traditional typology of seven firesetters (Fineman, 1995) was somewhat limiting in analyzing the data. However, the five categories were helpful in reviewing developmental and recidivistic differences in juvenile firesetters.

Future researchers may want to consider using a more simplistic triad that was supported by this dataset: non-pathological accidental, non-pathological cry-for-help, and pathological. Patterson's (1982) assertion that firesetters of different types and ages require different explanations for their firesetting was supported by this study. Also, because the FEMA forms appear to be limited in investigating non-pathological types of firesetters, items must be identified that better differentiate non-pathological from pathological types.

Implications of Findings on Future Research

It is interesting to note that fires set by juveniles account for a large portion of fire-related public property damage and deaths, but that these crimes received little attention in the literature or in the press. Because of the costs and impact of juvenile firesetting, developmentalists and mental health professionals need to continue to examine this behavior. Though efforts to understand and reduce firesetting are increasing, further efforts need to be taken to examine them from developmental perspectives that include individual as well as environmental factors. Researchers would be wise to identify methodologies that can assist in examining how peer, school, and family settings can impact whether and how juveniles use fire.

Firesetting can be classified as one of many examples of problem behavior that has been identified in juveniles. As with most juvenile problem behaviors, an examination of the particular characteristics and experiences of juveniles within the contexts can explain firesetting defined by a larger society or culture. In order for professionals and the Federal Emergency Management Agency to understand this problem behavior, clearer analysis of the home environment must exist.

Though the research on juvenile firesetting also has been subject to methodological and statistical limitations, it would appear that the results of this study agree largely with those that have preceded it. However, the breadth of the sample under study provided some interesting insights into how different types of firesetters differ in their firesetting based on levels of pathology, social skills, and delinquency.

Even more critical in understanding and intervening on the behalf of these juveniles is the impact of age, gender, and (even perhaps) race (more likely, differences based on socioeconomic status). Finding few differences based on gender helps to alleviate questions that firesetting is a behavior defined by gender (there is evidence in this study to suggest that a fair share of juvenile females use fire maladaptively as well). Some differences based on gender and race were statistically significant, and were believed to result from socializing agents in the environment. It could be that the implicit stereotyping of African-American youth in inner-city settings as deviant, or the greater chance for females to be identified as "needing help" led to such results. Future examinations of environments with which firesetters interact may assist in understanding these differences.

Researchers have questioned what dependent variable should be investigated in reviewing the behaviors of firesetters. The researcher used the following as dependent variables: (1) the magnitude of fire damage (based in dollar amount lost due to fire), (2) the presence of recidivism, and (3) the typology of firesetters. Because of the skewed nature of the magnitude of fire damage (most fireplay by juveniles does not result in any financial damage), fire professionals may find it helpful to investigate recidivism or the type of firesetter. Failure to investigate this developmental phenomena using the firesetting types implies a singularity about firesetting in children and adolescents (as performed in previous research) weakens our understanding of this phenomena.

Future Examinations of Juvenile Firesetting

It is an interest of this researcher to investigate juvenile firesetting as one form of juvenile behavior that can be used for four primary reasons: 1) as an expression of early childhood curiosity or adolescent experimentation, 2) as a plea for adult intervention during times of crisis, 3) as a challenge to authority, or 4) as a sign of psychopathology. As a developmentalist interested in the interplay between schools and families, it would be interesting to investigate the following topics related to juvenile firesetting:

Deviance and violence in youth. As with the results of this investigation, Loeber and Stouthamer-Loeber (1998) found that there is a discontinuous relationship between early childhood aggression and aggression in early adulthood. The authors also found that not all forms of violence have their origins in early childhood. The authors suggest that violent behaviors and aggressive attitudes need to be examined as they relate to the age of onset, time involved in the duration of the aggressive attitude, and age of the reduction of aggression (Loeber & Stouthamer-Loeber, 1998; also see Loeber, Keenan, & Zhang, 1997). It would be interesting to identify the average age of onset, time involved in the duration of firesetting, and the age of the reduction of the firesetting for each type of firesetter.

Delinquency, firesetting, and leisure time. Junger and Wiegersma (1995) examined the relationship between mild deviance and involvement in accidents, as well as common correlates of the two. Mild deviance was described in terms of gambling, drinking, smoking, soft-drug use, shoplifting, and vandalism, which are common examples of delinquent behavior. Results show that mild deviance was related most closely with leisure time activities. It would be interesting to examine how youth with few leisure time activities may be more likely to engage in firesetting, and what role peers, schools, or parents play in such behaviors.

Descriptors surrounding delinquent firesetting. A more qualitative interest that stems from these results is similar to the work of Heaven (1994), who examined why juvenile delinquents think they engage in delinquent behaviors. Heaven (1994) found that adolescents who were self-described as delinquent were more likely to engage in violent, sensation-seeking, and aggressive behaviors. It would be interesting to note why firesetters choose use of fire over other forms of delinquent acts.

Parental influence on social skills. Results indicate that firesetters tend to have conduct problems, such as disobedience and aggressiveness as a result of difficulty expressing feelings (Forehand et al., 1991; Thomas & Grimes, 1994). Children and adolescents who set fires are identified as having poor social awareness and limited ability or opportunity to express themselves. Sakheim, Vidgor, Gordon, and Helprin (1985) also found that firesetters had feelings of anger and resentment over parental rejection, and that such feelings largely were expressed covertly through the use of fire. By observing interactions between firesetters and significant adult models (e.g. – parents, family members, teachers, neighbors), perhaps a relationship can be identified between weak modeling of externalization of emotions and inappropriate juvenile use of fire.

School problems and firesetting. At the present time, limited information exists about firesetters' experiences with school and its importance as a socializing agent. It is an interest of future research to examine the importance of school peers and teachers as they might influence the behaviors of firesetters.

Identity problems and firesetting. It also has been theorized that some young adults initiate firesetting as they attempt to accommodate adult roles and acquire a sense of control. Recidivism in adolescent firesetters has been associated with feelings of inability to control one's environment or aspects of one's life (locus of control) (Kolko & Kazdin, 1994; Kolko, Kazdin, & Meyer, 1985). Though firesetting in adolescents and young adults is often associated with maladaptive psychosocial patterns, by early adulthood, most firesetters are identified as being pathological or criminals (Levin, 1976; Schwartzman et al., 1994). Perhaps older adolescents engage in such behaviors not for delinquent or cry for help purposes, but to assist in reformulating who they are as individuals.

Sociocultural theory and firesetting. Previous literature reviews of this subject have questioned whether some firesetters use fire to destroy home or school property because of anger or frustration with their communities or marginalization. The researcher would be interested in studying how aberrant behavior, such as firesetting, is the result of juveniles suffering from weak or nonexistent bonds to society, which causes them to behave in socially unacceptable ways.

Summary

An examination of the literature to date on firesetters shows that a variety of different characteristics can define specific types of firesetters. Furthermore, firesetting appear to differ as a result of both maturational factors and environmental factors. Future reviews of this subject should include an examination of the firesetter's history; such as with prior fire learning experiences, cognitive and behavioral reviews, and parent and family influences and stressors.

References

Achenbach, T.M. (1966). The classification of children's psychiatric symptoms: A factor analytic study. Psychological Monographs, 80, 615-632.

Adler, R., Nunn, R., Northam, E., Lebnan, V. (1994). Secondary prevention of early childhood firesetting. Journal of the American Academy of Child and Adolescent Psychiatry, 33, 1194-1202.

Bandura, A. (1977). Social learning theory. Engelwood Cliffs, NJ: Prentice Hall.

Barnett, W., & Spitzer, M. (1994). Pathological firesetting 1951-1991: A Review. Medicine Science and the Law, 34, 4-20.

Barnett, W., Richter, P., Sigmund, D., & Spitzer, M. (1997). Recidivism and concomitant criminality in pathological firesetters. Journal of Forensic Sciences, 42, 879-883.

Blumenberg, N.H. (1981). Arson update: A review of the literature on firesetting. Bulletin of the American Academy of Psychiatry and the Law, 9, 255-265.

Bronfenbrenner, U. (1977). Ecological systems theory. In R. Vasta (Ed.) Annals of child development (Vol 6). Greenwich, CT: JAI Press.

Bronfenbrenner, U. (1979). The ecology of human development. Cambridge, MA: Harvard University Press.

Bumpass, E.R., Fagelman, F.D., & Brix, R.J. (1983). Intervention with children who set fires. American Journal of Psychotherapy, 37, 328-345.

Burgess, R., & Akers, R. (1966). A differential association reinforcement theory of criminal behavior. Social Problems, 14, 128-147.

Canter, D., & Frizon, K. (1998). Differentiating arsonists: A model of firesetting actions and characteristics. Legal and Criminological Psychology, 3, 73-96.

Carey, K.T. (1997). Preschool interventions. In A.P. Goldstein & J.C. Conoley (Eds.) School violence intervention: A practical handbook. (pp. 93-106). New York, NY: Guilford Press.

Cohen, S. (1989). Sociological approaches to vandalism. In C. Levy-Leboyer (Ed.) Vandalism, behavior and motivation. New York: Elsworth.

Daderman, A., & af-Klinteberg, B. (1997). Personality dimensions characterizing severely conduct disordered male juvenile delinquents. Reports from the Department of Psychology – University of Stockholm, 831, 1-21.

DeSalvatore, G., & Hornstein, R. (1991). Juvenile firesetting: Assessment and treatment in psychiatric hospitalization and residential placement. Child and Youth Care Forum, 20, 103-114.

Donovan, J.E., & Jessor, R. (1978). Adolescent problem drinking: Psychosocial correlates in a national sample study. Journal of Studies on Alcohol, 39, 1506-1524.

Donovan, J.E., & Jessor, R. (1985). Structure of problem behavior in adolescence and young adulthood. Journal of Consulting and Clinical Psychology, 53, 890-904.

Eisler, R.M. (1972). Crisis intervention in the family of a firesetter. Psychotherapy-Theory, Research, and Practice, 9, 76-79.

Eysenck, H.J. (1994). Personality theory and the problem of criminality. In D.P. Farrington (Ed.) Psychological explanations of crime. The international library of criminology, criminal justice, & penology. (pp. 69-92). Aldershot, England: Dartmouth Publishing Company.

Federal Emergency Management Agency (1988). Child firesetter handbook. Washington, DC: United States Fire Administration.

Federal Emergency Management Agency (1995). Socioeconomic factors and the incidence of fire. Washington, DC: United States Fire Administration and National Fire Data Center.

Federal Emergency Management Agency (1996). Interviewing and counseling juvenile firesetters. Washington, DC: U.S. Government Printing Office.

Fineman, K.R. (1980). Firesetting in early childhood and adolescence. Pediatric Clinics of North America, 3, 483-500.

Fineman, K.R. (1995). A model for the qualitative analysis of child and adult fire deviant behavior. American Journal of Forensic Psychology, 13, 31-60.

Fineman, K.R. (1997a). Family Fire Risk Interview Form. Washington, DC: Federal Emergency Management Agency.

Fineman, K.R. (1997b). Juvenile Fire Risk Interview Form. Washington, DC: Federal Emergency Management Agency.

Fineman, K.R. (1997c). Parent Fire Risk Questionnaire. Washington, DC: FEMA.

Forehand, R., Wierson, M., Frame, C.L., Kemptom, T., & Armistead, L. (1991). Juvenile firesetting: A unique syndrome or an advanced level of antisocial behavior? Behavior Research and Therapy, 29, 125-128.

Freud, S. (1932). Original papers: The acquisition of power over fire. International Journal of Psychoanalysis, October 1932, 51 – 98.

Freud, S. (1930). Civilization and its Discontents. New York: W.W. Norton and Company.

Gaynor, J., & Hatcher, C. (1987). The psychology of child firesetting: Detection and intervention. New York: Bruner/Mazel.

Goldstein, A.P. (1996). The psychology of vandalism. New York, NY: Plenum Press.

Goldstein, A.P. (1997). Controlling vandalism: The person-environment duet. In A.P. Goldstein & J.C. Conoley (Eds.) School violence intervention: A practical handbook. (pp. 290-321). New York: Guilford Press.

Grolnick, W.S., Cole, R.E., Laurentis, L., & Schwartzman, P. (1990). Playing with fire: A developmental assessment of children's fire understanding and experience. Journal of Clinical Child Psychology, 19, 128-135.

Hanson, M., MacKay, S., Atkinson, L., Staley, S. (1994). Delinquent firesetters: A comparative study of delinquency and firesetting histories. Canadian Journal of Psychiatry, 39, 230-232.

Hanson, M., MacKay, S., Atkinson, L., Staley, S. (1995). Firesetting during the preschool period: Assessment and intervention issues. Special issue: Child and adolescent psychiatry. Canadian Journal of Psychiatry, 40, 299-303.

Harris, G.T., & Rice, M.E. (1996). A typology of mentally disordered firesetters. Journal of Interpersonal Violence, 11, 351-363.

Heath, G.A., Gayton, W.F., & Hardesty, V.A. (1976). Early childhood firesetting. Canadian Psychiatric Association Journal, 21, 229-237.

Heaven, P.C.L. (1994). Family of origin, personality, and self-reported delinquency. Journal of Adolescence, 17, 445-459.

Heller, M.S., Ehrlich, S.M., & Lester, D. (1984). Early childhood cruelty to animals, firesetting and enuresis as correlates of competence to stand trial. Journal of General Psychology, 110, 151-153.

Jackson, H.F., Glass, C., & Hope, S. (1987). A functional-analysis of recidivistic arson. British Journal of Clinical Psychology, 26, 175-185.

Jackson, H.F., Hope, S., & Glass, C. (1987). Why are arsonists not violent offenders? International Journal of Offender Therapy and Comparative Criminology, 31, 143-151.

Jessor, R. (1981). The perceived environment in psychological theory and research. In D. Magnusson (Ed.) Toward a psychology of situations: An interactional perspective, (pp. 297-317). New York: Lawrence Erlbaum Associates.

Jessor, R. (1987). Problem-behavior theory, psychosocial development, and adolescent problem drinking. British Journal of Addiction, 82, 331-342.

Jessor, R., Chase, J.A., & Donovan, J.E. (1980). Psychosocial correlates of marijuana use and problem drinking in a national sample of adolescents. American Journal of Public Health, 70, 604-613.

Jessor, R., Graves, T.D., Hanson, R.C., & Jessor, S.L. (1968). Society, personality, and deviant behavior: A study of a tri-ethnic community. New York: Holt, Rinehart, & Winston.

Jessor, R., & Jessor, S.L. (1973). The perceived environment in behavioral science: Some conceptual issues and some illustrative data. American Behavioral Scientist, 16, 801-828.

Jessor, R., & Jessor, S.L. (1977). Problem behavior and psychosocial development: A longitudinal study of youth. New York: Academic press.

Jessor, R., & Jessor, S.L. (1984). Adolescence to young adulthood: a 12-year prospective study of problem behavior and psychosocial development. In S.A. Mednick, M. Harway, & K.M. Finello (Eds.) Handbook of longitudinal research, Volume 2.

Jones, R.T., Ribbe, D.P., & Cunningham, P. (1994). Psychosocial correlates of fire disaster among children and adolescents. Journal of Traumatic Stress, 7, 117-122.

Junger, M., & Wiegersma, A. (1995). The relations between accidents, deviance and leisure time. Criminal Behavior and Mental Health, 53, 144-174.

Justice, B., Justice, R., & Kraft, I.A. (1974). Early warning signs of violence: Is a triad enough? American Journal of Psychiatry, 131, 457-459.

Kaufman, I., Heims, L.W., & Reiser, D.E. (1961). A re-evaluation of the psychodynamics of firesetting. American Journal of Orthopsychiatry, 31, 123-136.

Kazdin, A.E. (1990). Conduct disorder in early childhood. In M. Hersen & C.G. Last (Eds.) Handbook of child and adult psychopathology: A longitudinal perspective, (pp. 89-121). New York: Pergamon Press.

Kolko, D.J. (1983). Multicomponent parental treatment of firesetting in a six-year old boy. Journal of Behavioral Therapy and Experimental Psychiatry, 14, 349-353.

Kolko, D.J. (1985). Juvenile firesetting: A review and methodological critique. Clinical Psychology Review, 5, 345-376.

Kolko, D.J., Kazdin, A.E., & Meyer, E.C. (1985). Aggression and psychopathology in early childhood firesetters: Parent and child reports. Journal of Consulting and Clinical Psychology, 53, 377-385.

Kolko, D.J., & Kazdin, A.E. (1986a). A conceptualization of firesetting in children and adolescents. Journal of Abnormal Child Psychology, 14, 49-61.

Kolko, D.J., & Kazdin, A.E. (1986b). Parent psychopathology and family functioning among early childhood firesetters. Journal of Abnormal Child Psychology, 14, 315-329.

Kolko, D.J., & Kazdin, A.E. (1988). Parent-child correspondence in identification of firesetting among child psychiatric patients. Journal of Child Psychology and Psychiatry and Allied Disciplines, 29, 175-184.

Kolko, D.J., & Kazdin, A.E. (1991). Motives of early childhood firesetters: Firesetting characteristics and psychological correlates. Journal of Child Psychology and Psychiatry, 32, 535-550.

Kolko, D.J., & Kazdin, A.E. (1992). The emergence and recurrence of child firesetting: A one-year prospective study. Journal of Abnormal Child Psychology, 20, 17-37.

Kolko, D.J., & Kazdin, A.E. (1994). Children's descriptions of their firesetting incidents: Characteristics and relationship to recidivism. Journal of the American Academy of Child and Adolescent Psychiatry, 33, 114-122.

Lee, M.I., & Miltenberger, R.G. (1996). School refusal behavior: Classification, assessment, and treatment issues. Education and Treatment of Children, 19, 474-486.

Lester, D. (1975). Firesetting. Corrective and Social Psychiatry and Journal of Behavior Technology, Methods, and Therapy, 21, 22-26.

Levin, B. (1976). Psychological characteristics of firesetters. Fire Journal, 70, 36-41.

Lewin, K. (1951). Field theory in social science. New York: Harper.

Loeber, R., DeLamatre, M.S., Keenan, K., & Zhang, Q. (1998). A prospective replication of developmental pathways in disruptive and delinquent behavior. In R.B. Cairns & L.R. Bergman (Eds.) Methods and models for studying the individual. (pp. 185-218). Thousand Oaks, CA: Sage Publications.

Loeber, R., Keenan, K., & Zhang, Q. (1997). Boys' experimentation and persistence in developmental pathways toward serious delinquency. Journal of Child and Family Studies, 6, 321-357.

Loeber, R., & Stouthamer-Loeber, M. (1998). Development of juvenile aggression and violence: Some current misconceptions and controversies. American Psychologist, 53, 242-259.

Lowenstein, L.F. (1989). The etiology, diagnosis, and treatment of firesetting behavior of children. Child Psychiatry and Human Development, 19, 186-194.

Luby, J.L., Reich, W., & Earls, F. (1995). Failure to detect signs of psychological distress in the preschool children of alcoholic parents. Journal of Child and Adolescent Substance Abuse, 4, 77-89.

Macht, L.B., & Mack, J.E. (1968). The firesetter syndrome. Psychiatry, 31, 277-288.

Magnusson, D., & Endler, N.S. (1977). Personality at the crossroads: Current issues in interactional psychology. New York: Lawrence Erlbaum Associates.

Moore, J.M., Thompson-Pope, S.K., & Whited, R.M. (1996). MMPI-A: Profiles of adolescent boys with a history of firesetting. Journal of Personality Assessment, 67, 116-126.

Murphy, G.H., & Claire, I.C.H. (1996). Analysis of motivation in people with mild learning disabilities (mental handicap) who set fires. Psychology Crime and Law, 2, 153-164.

National Fire Protection Association (1999). Statistics on the national fire problem. Citation found at http://www.fema.gov/nfpa/.

Nielsen, G., Harrington, L., Sack, W.H., & Iatham, S. (1985). A developmental study of aggression and self-destruction in adolescents who received residential treatment. International Journal of Offender Therapy and Comparative Criminology, 29, 211-226.

Nunnally, J.C. (1994). Psychometric theory (3rd Edition). New York: McGraw Hill.

Patterson, G. (1982). A social learning approach (Vol 1). Eugene, OR: Castilia.

Prentky, R.A., & Carter, D.L. (1984). The predictive value of the triad for sex offenders. Behavioral Sciences and the Law, 2, 341-354.

Quinsey, V.L., Chaplin, T.C., & Upfold, D. (1989). Arsonists and sexual arousal to fire setting: Correlation unsupported. Journal of Behavior Therapy and Experimental Psychiatry, 20, 203-209.

Rachal, J.V., Guess, L.L., Hubbard, R.L., Maistro, S.A., Cavanaugh, E.R., Waddell, R, & Benrud, C.H. (1980). Adolescent drinking behavior. The extent and nature of adolescent alcohol and drug use: The 1974 and 1978 national sample studies. Triangle Park, NC: Research Triangle Institute.

Raine, A., Reynolds, C., Venables, P.H., Mednick, S.A., & Farrington, D.P. (1998). Fearlessness, stimulation-seeking, and large body size at age 3 years as early predispositions to early childhood aggression at age 11 years. Archives of General Psychiatry, 55, 745-751.

Raines, J.C., & Foy, C.W. (1994). Extinguishing the fires within: Treating juvenile firesetters. Families in Society: The Journal of Contemporary Human Services, 75, 595-607.

Repo, E., & Virkkunen, R.E. (1997). Young arsonists: History of conduct disorder, psychiatric diagnoses and criminal recidivism. Journal of Forensic Psychiatry, 8, 311-320.

Rice, M.E., & Harris, G.T. (1996). Predicting the recidivism of mentally disordered firesetters. Journal of Interpersonal Violence, 11, 364-375.

Robbins, E., & Robbins, L. (1967). Arson: With special reference to pyromania. New York State Journal of Medicine, 67, 795-798.

Rothstein, R. (1963). Explorations of ego structures of firesetting children. Archives of General Psychiatry, 9, 246-253.

Sakheim, G.A., & Osborn, E. (1999). Severe versus nonsevere firesetters revisited. Child Welfare, 78, 411-434.

Sakheim, G.A., Osborn, E., & Abrams, D. (1991). Toward a clearer differentiation of high-risk from low-risk firesetters. Child Welfare, 70, 489-503.

Sakheim, G.A., Vidgor, M.C., Gordon, M., & Helprin, L.M. (1985). A psychological profile of juvenile firesetters in residential treatment. Child Welfare, 64, 453-476.

Saunders, E.B., & Awad, G.A. (1991). Adolescent female firesetters. Special issue: Child and adolescent psychiatry. Canadian Journal of Psychiatry, 36, 401-404.

Schaenman, P., Hall, Schainblatt, R., Swartz, A., & Karter, E. (1977). Procedures for improving the measurement of local fire protection effectiveness. Boston: National Fire Protection Association: pp. 53-71.

Schwartzman, P., Stambaugh, H., & Kimball, J. (1994). Arson and juveniles: Responding to the violence. A review of teen firesetting and interventions (Federal Emergency Management Agency – United States Fire Administration). Emmitsburg, Maryland: United States Fire Administration.

Showers, J., & Pickrell, E. (1987). Child firesetters: A study of three populations. Hospital and Community Psychiatry, 38, 495-501.

Spurlin, B. (1999, June 16). Personnel communication regarding Fire Stop Program protocol (B. Spurlin – Marion County Fire Stop Program). Indianapolis, IN: Marion County Fire Stop.

Squires, T. & Busuttil, A. (1995). Child fatalities in Scottish house fires: 1980-1990: A case of child neglect? Child Abuse and Neglect, 19, 865-873.

State Emergency Management Agency (1999). Personal communication regarding Marion County statistics (B. Spurlin – Marion County Fire Stop Program 1998 Annual Report). Indianapolis, IN: Marion County Fire Stop.

Stewart, M.A., & Culver, K.W. (1982). Children who start fires: The clinical picture and a follow-up. British Journal of Psychiatry, 140, 357-363.

Swaffer, T., & Hollin, C.R.(1995). Adolescent firesetting: Why do they say they do it? Journal of Adolescence, 18, 619-623.

Taylor, J.C., & Carr, E.G. (1994). Severe problem behaviors of children with developmental disabilities: Reciprocal social influences. In T. Thompson & D. Gray (Eds). Destructive behavior in developmental disabilities: Diagnosis and treatment, (pp. 274-289). Thousand Oaks, CA: Sage Publications.

Thomas, A., & Grimes, J. (1994). Children's needs: Psychological Perspectives. Silver Spring, MD: National Association of School Psychologists.

Vandersall, T.A., & Wiener, J.M. (1970). Children who set fires. Archives of General Psychology, 22, 63-71.

Wax, D.E., & Haddox, V.G. (1974). Enuresis, fire setting, and animal cruelty: A useful danger signal in predicting vulnerability of adolescent males to assaultive behavior. Child Psychiatry and Human Development, 4, 151-156.

Williams, D. (1998). Delinquent and deliberate firesetters in the middle years of early childhood and adolescence. Dissertational Abstracts, 1998, 1-121.

Winget, C.N., & Whitnam, R.M. (1973). Coping with problems: Attitudes toward children who set fires. American Journal of Psychiatry, 130, 442-445.

Yarnell, H. (1940). Firesetting in children. American Journal of Orthopsychiatry, 10, 272-287.

Appendix A

Family Fire Risk Interview Form (Fineman, 1997a)

Appendix B

Juvenile Fire Risk Interview Form (Fineman, 1997b)

Appendix C

Parent Fire Risk Questionnaire (Fineman, 1997c)

Appendix D

Characteristics Used to Define the Category of Firesetter

Category	Characteristics
Curiosity Type	engage in firesetting as experimentation
	often show remorse for their behaviors following the incident
	tend not to understand the consequences of their behaviors
	early involvement with firesetting
	start a fire in a desire to watch a flame
Accidental Type	teenagers engaging in experimental firesetting or those playing scientist
	young adult accidents or adult carelessness
	hold no intent to cause harm
"Cry for Help" Type	attempt to bring attention to their individual or familial dysfunction
	not thought to mean to cause harm or damage
	inability to appropriately express themselves
	set fires in order to be seen as would be hero types
	some history of abuse or neglect
Delinquent Type	set fire for profit and those that set fire to cover another
	have an interest in vandalism and hate crimes
	as child firesetters, this group shows some empathy for others
	as adolescent firesetters show little empathy for others
	higher rates of other deviant behaviors preceding firesetting

Appendix D

Characteristics Used to Define the Category of Firesetter

Category	Characteristics
Severely Disturbed Type	diagnosed by a wide variety of individual pathologies
	early signs as a result of individual psychopathology
	more likely to be found in an inpatient population
	high incidents of recidivism
	may be paranoid
	pyromaniac is a sub-type of the severely disturbed category
Cognitively Impaired Type	diagnoses such as attention deficit disorder (ADD), attention deficit hyperactivity disorder (ADHD), learning disabled (LD), or mildly mentally retarded (MMR), as well as those youth who are retarded or have some organic brain dysfunction.
	also included in this group are persons with severe learning disabilities, those affected by fetal alcohol syndrome, or by drugs taken by their mother during pregnancy.
Sociocultural Type	young adult or adult arsonists
	set fires primarily for the support they get for doing so by groups
	typically are in the midst of civil unrest
	enraged or enticed by the activity of others and follow suit
	set fires with deliberation in order to call attention to their cause

Appendix E

Appendix of Terms

Abuse - A series of harmful behaviors and actions as defined by local law that places an individual at risk requires reporting. See Section 7-2 NFPA 1035-Proposed.

Accident - An unplanned event that interrupts an activity and sometimes causes injury or damage. A chance occurrence arising from unknown causes; an unexpected happening due to carelessness, ignorance, and the like. NFPA 921 1998 Edition.

Accidental firesetter - This type of firesetter usually involves children under the age of 11 years. It also may include teenagers playing scientist. The fire results from no destructive motive to create fire (Fineman, 1995).

Arson - The crime of maliciously and intentionally, or recklessly starting a fire or causing an explosion. Precise legal definitions vary among jurisdictions, wherein it is defined by statutes and judicial decisions. NFPA 921 1998 Edition.

CHINS - Child in need of service. There are numerous elements to Indiana's legal definition. See Section 7-2; NFPA 1035-Proposed.

Cognitively Impaired firesetter (Include diagnosis of ADD, ADHD, LD, MMR, etc.) - This type of firesetter includes the retarded and the mentally impaired individuals. These firesetters tend to avoid intention harm, but lack acceptable judgment. Significant property damage is common. Prognistically, they are acceptable therapy candidates. Also included in this group are persons with severe learning disabilities, those affected by fetal alcohol syndrome, or by drugs taken by their mother during pregnancy (Fineman, 1995).

Confidentiality - Principle that recognizes the privacy of individuals (within limits) of law and professional ethics. See Section 7-2; NPFA 1035-Proposed.

Core Intervention - Programs that provide long-term help for juvenile firesetters and their families to eliminate firesetting behavior and remediate the accompanying psychopathology. See Section 7-2; NFPA 1035-Proposed.

The "Cry for Help" firesetter - Include diagnosis of ADHD, Depression NOS, Major Depression, ODD, PTSD. This type of firesetter includes those offenders whom consciously or subconsciously wish to bring attention to an interpersonal dysfunction (depression) to an interpersonal dysfunction (abuse at home, vicarious observation of parental conflict). The use of fire or firesetting is not meant to harm people. These juveniles have a acceptable prognosis for treatment. A subsection of this type is the firefighter who sets fires or adult/juvenile "would be hero types" - seeking the attention of peers or the community in order to discover or help put out fires they start. The "cry for help" type is the traditional early childhood diagnosis for abused individuals (Fineman, 1995).

Juvenile Firesetters: An Exploratory Analysis 163

Curiosity firesetter - Typically this firesetter is younger children, who do not understand the consequences of their behavior. The motivation to fireset is the desire is to watch the flame. There is generally no intent to cause harm. The curiosity firesetter is the traditional early childhood diagnosis. Hyperactivity or an attention deficit may be present (Fineman, 1995).

Custodian - A person with whom a child resides. See Section 7-2; NFPA 1035-Proposed.

Delinquent firesetter (Adolescent) or Antisocial firesetter (Adult) - The delinquent or antisocial firesetter includes the fire for profit type and the cover another crime type. These firesetters' interest in vandalism and hate crimes is noteworthy. As juveniles, this type shows little empathy for others, and shows little conscious. Juvenile types rarely harms others with fire, but significant property damage is common. As adults, a significant percentage of these firesetters harm others. Firesetting behavior is more easily extinguished than other personality and behavior problems, which usually accompany the firesetting (Fineman, 1995).

Early Intervention - Programs aimed to identify children at risk for participating in unsupervised firesetting and firesetting incidents. See Section 7-2; NFPA 1035-Proposed.

Firesetting - No actual fire set. Firesetting may progress to firesetting and should therefore be addressed as early and rapidly as possible. See Section 7-2; NFPA 1035-Proposed.

Firesetting - Any unsanctioned, noninstructional use of fire involvement, including both intentional and unintentional involvement, whether or not an actual fire occurred. See Section 7-2; NFPA 1035-Proposed.

Foster Parent - An individual who provide care and supervision to a child, a foster home, or a home approved as a foster home. See Section 7-2; NFPA 1035-Proposed.

Guardian - A person appointed by a court to have the care and custody of a child or the child's estate, or both. See Section 7-2; NFPA 1035-Proposed.

Incendiary Fire - The incendiary fire is deliberately ignited under circumstances in which the person knows that the fire should not be ignited. NFPA 921 1998 Edition; See Section 12-2.3.

Intake forms - Consistent body of information collected about an individual as a prerequisite to intervention. See Section 7-2; NFPA 1035-Proposed.

Intentionally - Person's conscious objective to do the act. See Section 7-2; NFPA 1035-Proposed. NFPA 921 1998 Edition; See Section 12-2.3.

Interagency network - A group of agencies (public safety, social services, education, mental health, law enforcement, and juvenile justice) working a formal partnership to address juvenile firesetting. See Section 7-2; NFPA 1035-Proposed.

Intervention - Formal response to firesetting behavior that may include evaluation and education, counseling, medial, social services, and juvenile justice sanctions. See Section 7-2; NFPA 1035-Proposed.

Interview - A structured process by which relevant information is gathered for the purpose of determining specific intervention. See Section 7-2; NFPA 1035-Proposed.

Juvenile - A person who is under eighteen years of age. NFPA 921 1998 Edition; See Section 12-2.3.

Knowingly - If the act is willed and is done with an awareness of the probable consequences. See Section 7-2; NFPA 1035-Proposed.

Neglect - Failure to act on behalf of or in protection of an individual in your care. See Section 7-2; NFPA 1035-Proposed.

Parent - A biological or adoptive caregiver. Unless otherwise specified, it includes both parents, regardless of their marital status. See Section 7-2; NFPA 1035-Proposed.

Primary prevention - Programs aimed at reducing juvenile involvement in first-time unsupervised firesetting and firesetting incidents. See Section 7-2; NFPA 1035-Proposed.

Referral - An act or process by which a juvenile firesetter and family gain access to a program. See Section 7-2; NFPA 1035-Proposed.

Severely Disturbed firesetter - This category of firesetter includes paranoid and psychotic types for whom the fixation of fire may be a major factor in the development of a mental disorder. Sensory aspects of the fire (e.g. - the flame, smoke, the heat produced) are sufficiently reinforcing to cause fires to be frequently set. Pyromaniac is a sub-type - sensory reinforcement is often powerful enough for significant harm to occur. Self-harm type uses fire to harm or kill himself/herself. Prognosis is guarded with this group (Fineman, 1995).

Sociocultural firesetter - The sociocultural firesetter includes the uncontrolled "mass hysteria type," the attention to cause harm type, the religious type, and the satanic type. These are generally arsonists who set fires primarily for the support they get for doing so by groups within their communities. They also are those who may set fires in the midst of civil unrest, and are either enraged and enticed by the activity of others and follow suit, or set fires with deliberation in order to call attention to the righteousness of their cause. They frequently lose control and harm others. Treatment is often guarded with this group (Fineman, 1995).

Appendix E

Coding Manual for Marion County Arson Investigation Network Datafile

Data Gathering Protocol

The purpose of this appendix is to summarize the protocol used by MCAIN to collect the data subsequently used in the present study. The sequence of the data gathering protocol included the following stages: (a) the firesetting event, (b) the investigation of the firesetting event by professionals, (c) the fire site interview by professionals, (d) referral by fire professionals to the Fire Stop psychoeducational program with MCAIN, and (e) the Fire Stop program interview. The Fire Stop program interview included an interview of family members using the Family Fire Risk Interview Form (Fineman, 1997a), the Juvenile Fire Risk Interview Form (Fineman, 1997b), and the Parent Fire Risk Questionnaire (Fineman, 1997c).

Firesetting Event

Firesetting events were operationalized as any occurrence of fire in which a juvenile was identified as engaging in firesetting. Fire professionals were contacted about firesetting events by several referral sources, including parents, neighbors, school personnel, and mental health professionals. Fire professionals visited the event site within 90 minutes of the referral. Fires that were investigated by MCAIN have originated at a variety of sites; including homes, schools, abandoned buildings, abandoned cars, alleyways, and trash dumpsters.

Fire Site Evaluation

Initial information regarding a firesetting event was obtained during a site survey. Site surveys and initial fire site interviews were performed at the locale where the fire occurred. Fire professionals included either arson investigators or police officers with the juvenile justice system. Fire professionals were certified to perform arson investigations following training with the Indiana State Fire Marshal's Office and/or the United States Fire Administration.

Fire professionals were responsible for completing a standard arson investigation form designed by the Federal Emergency Management Agency (FEMA, 1988). Information regarding the youth's firesetting was taken from interviews performed at the site of the fire. Investigators collected statements from the juvenile firesetter(s), their family members, and other witnesses of the fire. Investigators also completed an estimated dollar amount of property loss as a result of the juvenile's firesetting.

Referral to Fire Stop Program

Following the arson investigation, the fire professional referred the juvenile to the Fire Stop program with MCAIN. Referrals were made to the Fire Stop program if the firesetter was between the ages of 3 years and 18 years old at the time of the event. Juveniles and their parents scheduled appointments with the director of MCAIN's Fire Stop program within 10 days of the firesetting event. Secondary information also was identified during a follow-up interview at the MCAIN headquarters during a psychoeducational intervention, the Fire Stop Program. Juvenile firesetters were most likely to have been referred by fire professionals following the fire site interviews.

However, firesetters also could have been referred by other professionals, such as teachers, school counselors, physicians, counselors, social workers, or state caseworkers. If referral was performed by a professional other than a fire professional, the standard arson investigation form was completed by the Fire Stop program staff. Data points collected during the referral were general demographic information about the firesetter and their family. Demographic variables were added to the information obtained during the fire site evaluation.

Fire Stop Program staff. The Marion County Arson Investigation Network Fire Stop Program is headed by a fire professional with over 30 years experience, and was the first professional in Indiana to initiate a state-run psychoeducation program for firesetters in 1984. Prior to her work with psychoeducation, she was an arson investigator for Wayne Township Fire Department for 21 years. She has served as a facilitator for the United States Fire Administration certification committee for arson investigation education, and is a member of the Indiana State Fire Marshal's Office Juvenile Firesetter Committee.

Fire Stop Program curriculum. The MCAIN Fire Stop Program includes secondary investigation of the firesetting event, as well as a 3-hour psychoeducational intervention program for juvenile firesetters and their families. In addition to completion of a fire risk evaluation (see Fineman, 1997a, 1997b, 1997c), the Fire Stop program provides incident-specific and age-appropriate education for firesetters and their family. Data used in the present study included information taken during the secondary investigation of the firesetting event as well as the psychoeducational intervention program. Data points included are any information completed on the FEMA Fire Risk Evaluation forms (Fineman, 1997a, 1997b, 1997c), as well as a separate narrative record provided by the Fire Stop director.

Fire Stop Program Interview

After arriving for their scheduled interview at the Marion County Arson Investigation Unit Headquarters, parents and children entered an office that included a large table surrounded by chairs. The office included pictures on surrounding walls espousing information on fire prevention. The table was cleared, except for the juvenile's data record and blank interview forms. A videorecorder was stationed in the corner, which would later be used for the psychoeducational portion of the program.

Data collection took place during a scheduled three-hour interview between the fire professional, the firesetter, and the firesetter's parent/guardian following referral to the MCAIN Fire Stop program. For most subjects juvenile firesetters were accompanied by their biological mothers. Few interviews were identified that included both parents, and few interviews were identified where children were brought in by male guardians or fathers. Interview protocol follows the recommended interview format designed by the Federal Emergency Management Agency (FEMA, 1988). Participants and their parents completed questionnaires and interview questions as fulfillment of mandatory program requirements. Parents and participants were told that they were to engage in a brief discussion regarding their firesetting behaviors.

Following referral to the program, a MCAIN data record was created for the juvenile firesetter. Each data record of the MCAIN database includes demographic information, the nature of the firesetter's behaviors, the firesetting incident, and whether or not the individual followed-up with any counseling following the fire. Four primary pieces of information are included in each data record: (a) the narrative information taken from the fire site interview, (b) the Family Fire Risk Interview Form (Fineman, 1997a), (c) the Juvenile Fire Risk Interview Form (Fineman, 1997b), and (d) the Parent Fire Risk Questionnaire (Fineman, 1997c). Psychometric data for each of these forms is included in Chapter Four of this document.

Family Fire Risk Interview Form. First, parents and juveniles completed the Family Fire Risk Interview Form (Fineman, 1997a, see Appendix A). The director of the Fire Stop Program was responsible for reading off questions from the interview form in a semi-structured format. The director indicated that most questions during this time are answered by the parent/guardian, but juveniles are able to interject their ideas and beliefs during the interview (Spurlin, 1999, personal communication). Completion time for this 65-question interview form was approximately 30 minutes.

The Family Fire Risk Interview Form includes two scales, a Parent Scale and a Child Scale. Responses made by parents are included on the scale for parents. Responses made by juveniles are included on the scale for children. The questionnaire includes 65 questions in Likert Scale format. Each scale ranges from 1 (Rarely to never) to 3 (Frequently), parents were required to answer statements such as [my child has] "learning problems at school," [my child is] "physically violent," and [my child has] "curiosity about fire." Questions that are answered as occurring rarely to never (rating of 1) are coded as indicating little concern for recidivistic firesetting. Higher scores are an indication of psychosocial risk for recidivistic firesetting.

Juvenile Fire Risk Interview Form. Following completion of the Family Fire Risk Interview Form, the parent and juvenile are separated so that the juvenile could complete a second interview form. After the parent had left the room, the juvenile completed the Juvenile Fire Risk Interview Form (Fineman, 1997b, see Appendix B). The director of the Fire Stop Program was responsible for reading off questions from the interview form in a semi-structured format. Completion time for this 65-question interview form was approximately 45 minutes.

The questionnaire includes 65 questions, some forced choice format questions and some questions in Likert Scale format. The Likert Scale questions used a scale ranging from 1 (Rarely to never) to 3 (Frequently), and juveniles were required to answer statements such as "Have you gotten in trouble at school?," "Do you think your friends are a bad influence on you?," and "Do you usually do things you are asked to do?." Higher scores are an indication of psychosocial risk for recidivistic firesetting.

Parent Fire Risk Questionnaire. Following completion of the Family Fire Risk Interview Form, parents were asked to leave the room to complete the Parent Fire Risk Questionnaire (Fineman, 1997c). Parents were provided assistance if they had difficulty understanding questions or reading the material provided to them. The questionnaires were filled out in a room adjacent to where their child was being interviewed. The questionnaire required approximately 20 minutes to complete.

The questionnaire includes 116 questions in Likert Scale format. Using a scale ranging from 1 (Rarely to never) to 3 (Frequently), parents were required to answer statements such as [my child has] "learning problems at school," [my child is] "physically violent," and [my child has] "curiosity about fire." Higher scores are an indication of psychosocial risk for recidivistic firesetting.

After completing the questionnaire, the parent and firesetters reunited and finished the interview section of the Fire Stop program by reviewing the information obtained. The information obtained during the interview is used to identify the likelihood of recidivist firesetting. Following completion of all interview materials, the Fire Stop facilitator tallies the responses on all three instruments. If the majority (over 80%) of the responses were of mild or moderate concern, an educational intervention would be appropriate. If the majority of the responses were of extreme concern, a referral to a mental health professional is required (FEMA, 1988).

Procedure

Creating a Data File

An electronic dataset separate from the MCAIN datafile was created using the MCAIN records. Information was organized from the MCAIN files into a separate database using the ACCESS data management system. No information was transferred directly from MCAIN computer files to the current study's computerized SPSS data file. In other words all data utilized in the present study was organized and entered by the researcher for the sole purpose of this investigation.

Each data record included a fire event narrative, a referral, the Fire Stop Interview narrative, and the Fineman instruments. In the event that a firesetter engages in recidivist behaviors, all information was included for each individual fire event. First, the MCAIN records for juvenile firesetters were accessed. MCAIN records are organized by month and year, and included juvenile firesetters from January 1994 to December 1999. For the purposes of this study, information was taken from juvenile firesetting records obtained from January 1994 through December 1999 as a result in revisions to the Federal Emergency Management Agency forms (Fineman, 1997a, 1997b, 1997c).

The records are housed in manila folders on site at MCAIN headquarters. Each manila folder contains demographic information, completed FEMA (Fineman, 1997a, 1997b, 1997c) forms, a narrative record from the preliminary on-site interviews taken at the time of the fire, and any correspondence between MCAIN staff and juvenile justice regarding the incident. Supplemental materials, such as juvenile court records on the individual and narrative notes made by the director also were included in a data record (Spurlin, 1999). Prior to recording data to the research data file, all identifying labels were expunged.

Decisions regarding the data. Only data records that include the FEMA (Fineman, 1997a, 1997b, 1997c) forms and the narrative record from the preliminary on-site interviews taken at the time of the fire were utilized. It was found that this included approximately 91% of all juveniles referred to the Fire Stop program. Files completed prior to the introduction of the revised FEMA (Fineman, 1997a, 1997b, 1997c) instruments were included in analysis for this study. Though the instruments were revised in 1997, these revisions were cosmetic in nature, and the wording of questions and organization of the questionnaires has remained the same since 1994.

Criteria for exclusion included blank FEMA (Fineman, 1997a, 1997b, 1997c) forms, an absence of the narrative record from the preliminary on-site interview, or a failure on the part of the MCAIN staff or parent/guardian to complete the necessary FEMA instruments. In the event that a file was missing a narrative record from the preliminary on-site interview, attempts were made to access police records that are likely to contain this narrative.

Missing data. Missing data were likely to result from questions that were neglected during the completion of the FEMA questionnaires. The missing responses would thus differently jeopardize the reliability of that record. In the event that an entire scale is missing from a questionnaire, the individual record was excluded from data analysis. In the event that individual questions were not completed on a questionnaire, but that a majority of the scale was completed, the median item value was substituted for the data point.

Miscoded data. Miscoded data included any computer data that does not match hard data taken from the MCAIN records, as well as any subscale score that is beyond the appropriate range for that scale. In the event that miscoded data were identified, it was recoded using information taken from the MCAIN file records. In the event that miscoded data could not be taken from the MCAIN records, values were identified by computer records held at the Marion County courthouse. Finally, when information could not be obtained by performing the previous methods, median values for those questions were used in the place of the miscoded data.

List of Variables in the Datafile

The following list of variables includes all the variables used in the MCAIN datafile for the present study. Information for each variable includes the name of the variable, the datafile coding name for the variable, examples and non examples of the variable (where pertinent), and any necessary information regarding the scales for the variable.

Date of Birth

    Coding name - DOB
    Information - day, month, and year of juvenile's birth

Age

    Coding name - AGE
    Information - chronological age of the juvenile based in months

Gender

> Coding name - SEX
> Information - biological sex of the juvenile
> Value labels -
>
> > 1.00 male
> > 2.00 female

Race

> Coding name - RACE
> Information - race of the juvenile
> Value labels -
>
> > 1.00 Caucasian-American
> > 2.00 African-American
> > 3.00 Hispanic-American
> > 4.00 Mixed
> > 5.00 Asian-American

Dollar Amount Lost to Fire

> Coding name - DOLLAR
> Information - dollar amount lost in property value as a result of the fire

Grade Level of Juvenile

> Coding name - GRADE
> Information - grade level/school level of juvenile

Female Caregiver to Juvenile

> Coding name - FCARE
> Information - primary female caregiver to juvenile
> Value labels -
>
> > 0.00 none
> > 1.00 biological mother
> > 2.00 adoptive mother
> > 3.00 grandmother
> > 4.00 aunt
> > 5.00 family friend
> > 6.00 sister

Female Caregiver's Marital Status

    Coding name - FMARSTAT
    Information - primary female caregiver's marital status
    Value labels -

        1.00   married
        2.00   separated
        3.00   divorced
        4.00   single
        5.00   widowed

Female Caregiver's Date of Birth

    Coding name - FDOB
    Information - day, month, and year of primary female caregiver's date of birth

Female Caregiver's Age

    Coding name - FCAREAGE
    Information - primary female caregiver's age in years

Female Caregiver's Employment Status

    Coding name - FEMPLOY
    Information - primary female caregiver's employment status
    Value labels -

        1.00   yes-full time
        2.00   yes-part time
        3.00   no
        4.00   incarcerated

Male Caregiver to Juvenile

    Coding name - MCARE
    Information - primary male caregiver to juvenile
    Value labels -

        0.00   none
        1.00   biological father
        2.00   adoptive father
        3.00   grandfather
        4.00   uncle
        5.00   family friend
        6.00   brother

Male Caregiver's Marital Status

Coding name - MMARSTAT
Information - primary male caregiver's marital status
Value labels -

- 1.00 married
- 2.00 separated
- 3.00 divorced
- 4.00 single
- 5.00 widowed

Male Caregiver's Date of Birth

Coding name - MDOB
Information - day, month, and year of primary male caregiver's date of birth

Male Caregiver's Age

Coding name - MCAREAGE
Information - primary male caregiver's age in years

Male Caregiver's Employment Status

Coding name - MEMPLOY
Information - primary male caregiver's employment status
Value labels -

- 1.00 yes-full time
- 2.00 yes-part time
- 3.00 no
- 4.00 incarcerated

Female Secondary Caregiver to Juvenile

Coding name - FNONCARE
Information - secondary female caregiver to juvenile
Value labels -

- 0.00 none
- 1.00 biological mother
- 2.00 adoptive mother
- 3.00 grandmother
- 4.00 aunt
- 5.00 family friend
- 6.00 sister

Female Secondary Caregiver's Marital Status

    Coding name - FNONMAR
    Information - secondary female caregiver's marital status
    Value labels -

        1.00   married
        2.00   separated
        3.00   divorced
        4.00   single
        5.00   widowed

Female Secondary Caregiver's Date of Birth

    Coding name - FNONDOB
    Information - day, month, and year of secondary female caregiver's date of birth

Female Secondary Caregiver's Age

    Coding name - FNONAGE
    Information - secondary female caregiver's age in years

Female Secondary Caregiver's Employment Status

    Coding name - FNONEMP
    Information - secondary female caregiver's employment status
    Value labels -

        1.00   yes-full time
        2.00   yes-part time
        3.00   no
        4.00   incarcerated

Male Secondary Caregiver to Juvenile

    Coding name - MNONCARE
    Information - secondary male caregiver to juvenile
    Value labels -

        0.00   none
        1.00   biological father
        2.00   adoptive father
        3.00   grandfather
        4.00   uncle
        5.00   family friend
        6.00   brother

Male Secondary Caregiver's Marital Status

Coding name - MNONMAR
Information - secondary male caregiver's marital status
Value labels -

    1.00   married
    2.00   separated
    3.00   divorced
    4.00   single
    5.00   widowed

Male Secondary Caregiver's Date of Birth

Coding name - MNONDOB
Information - day, month, and year of secondary male caregiver's date of birth

Male Secondary Caregiver's Age

Coding name - MNONAGE
Information - secondary male caregiver's age in years

Male Secondary Caregiver's Employment Status

Coding name - MNONEMP
Information - secondary male caregiver's employment status
Value labels -

    1.00   yes-full time
    2.00   yes-part time
    3.00   no
    4.00   incarcerated

Number of Other Juveniles in the Home

Coding name - INDVHOME
Information - number of other juvenile individuals in the home

Type of Juvenile Firesetter

    Coding name - TYPEFIRE
    Information - type of juvenile firesetter, based on categorization system
    Value labels -

        1.00   curious
        2.00   accidental
        3.00   cry for help
        4.00   delinquent
        5.00   severely disturbed
        6.00   cognitively impaired
        7.00   sociocultural type

FEMA Parent Fire Risk Questionnaire Variable 1

    Coding name - PFRQ1
    Information - hyperactivity at school
    Value labels -

        1.00   rarely to never
        2.00   sometimes
        3.00   frequently

FEMA Parent Fire Risk Questionnaire Variable 2

    Coding name - PFRQ2
    Information - lack of concentration
    Value labels -

        1.00   rarely to never
        2.00   sometimes
        3.00   frequently

FEMA Parent Fire Risk Questionnaire Variable 3

    Coding name - PFRQ3
    Information - learning problems at school
    Value labels -

        1.00   rarely to never
        2.00   sometimes
        3.00   frequently

FEMA Parent Fire Risk Questionnaire Variable 4

    Coding name - PFRQ4
    Information - behavior problems at school
    Value labels -

        1.00   rarely to never
        2.00   sometimes
        3.00   frequently

FEMA Parent Fire Risk Questionnaire Variable 5

    Coding name - PFRQ5
    Information - impulsive
    Value labels -

        1.00   rarely to never
        2.00   sometimes
        3.00   frequently

FEMA Parent Fire Risk Questionnaire Variable 6

    Coding name - PFRQ6
    Information - impatient
    Value labels -

        1.00   rarely to never
        2.00   sometimes
        3.00   frequently

FEMA Parent Fire Risk Questionnaire Variable 7

    Coding name - PFRQ7
    Information - fantasizes (day dreaming)
    Value labels -

        1.00   rarely to never
        2.00   sometimes
        3.00   frequently

FEMA Parent Fire Risk Questionnaire Variable 8

    Coding name - PFRQ8
    Information - likes school
    Value labels -

        1.00   rarely to never
        2.00   sometimes
        3.00   frequently

FEMA Parent Fire Risk Questionnaire Variable 9

    Coding name - PFRQ9
    Information - listens to teacher(s)/school authorities
    Value labels -

        1.00   rarely to never
        2.00   sometimes
        3.00   frequently

FEMA Parent Fire Risk Questionnaire Variable 10

    Coding name - PFRQ10
    Information - shows age appropriate interest in future school/jobs/career
    Value labels -

        1.00   rarely to never
        2.00   sometimes
        3.00   frequently

FEMA Parent Fire Risk Questionnaire Variable 11

    Coding name - PFRQ11
    Information - truant/school runaway
    Value labels -

        1.00   rarely to never
        2.00   sometimes
        3.00   frequently

FEMA Parent Fire Risk Questionnaire Variable 12

    Coding name - PFRQ12
    Information - convulsions/seizures/"spells"
    Value labels -

        1.00   rarely to never
        2.00   sometimes
        3.00   frequently

FEMA Parent Fire Risk Questionnaire Variable 13

    Coding name - PFRQ13
    Information - need for excessive security
    Value labels -

        1.00   rarely to never
        2.00   sometimes
        3.00   frequently

FEMA Parent Fire Risk Questionnaire Variable 14

    Coding name - PFRQ14
    Information - need for affection
    Value labels -

        1.00   rarely to never
        2.00   sometimes
        3.00   frequently

FEMA Parent Fire Risk Questionnaire Variable 15

    Coding name - PFRQ15
    Information - loss of appetite
    Value labels -

        1.00   rarely to never
        2.00   sometimes
        3.00   frequently

FEMA Parent Fire Risk Questionnaire Variable 16

    Coding name - PFRQ16
    Information - excessive weight loss
    Value labels -

        1.00   rarely to never
        2.00   sometimes
        3.00   frequently

FEMA Parent Fire Risk Questionnaire Variable 17

    Coding name - PFRQ17
    Information - excessive overweight
    Value labels -

        1.00   rarely to never
        2.00   sometimes
        3.00   frequently

FEMA Parent Fire Risk Questionnaire Variable 18

    Coding name - PFRQ18
    Information - knows what is moral
    Value labels -

        1.00   rarely to never
        2.00   sometimes
        3.00   frequently

FEMA Parent Fire Risk Questionnaire Variable 19

    Coding name - PFRQ19
    Information - feels acceptable about self
    Value labels -

        1.00   rarely to never
        2.00   sometimes
        3.00   frequently

FEMA Parent Fire Risk Questionnaire Variable 20

    Coding name - PFRQ20
    Information - comfortable with own body
    Value labels -

        1.00   rarely to never
        2.00   sometimes
        3.00   frequently

FEMA Parent Fire Risk Questionnaire Variable 21

    Coding name - PFRQ21
    Information - likes overall looks
    Value labels -

        1.00   rarely to never
        2.00   sometimes
        3.00   frequently

FEMA Parent Fire Risk Questionnaire Variable 22

    Coding name - PFRQ22
    Information - stuttering
    Value labels -

        1.00   rarely to never
        2.00   sometimes
        3.00   frequently

FEMA Parent Fire Risk Questionnaire Variable 23

    Coding name - PFRQ23
    Information - wets during the day (after age 3)
    Value labels -

        1.00   rarely to never
        2.00   sometimes
        3.00   frequently

FEMA Parent Fire Risk Questionnaire Variable 24

    Coding name - PFRQ24
    Information - night time bed wetting (after age 3)
    Value labels -

        1.00   rarely to never
        2.00   sometimes
        3.00   frequently

FEMA Parent Fire Risk Questionnaire Variable 25

    Coding name - PFRQ25
    Information - soiling
    Value labels -

        1.00   rarely to never
        2.00   sometimes
        3.00   frequently

FEMA Parent Fire Risk Questionnaire Variable 26

    Coding name - PFRQ26
    Information - is acceptable in sports
    Value labels -

        1.00   rarely to never
        2.00   sometimes
        3.00   frequently

FEMA Parent Fire Risk Questionnaire Variable 27

    Coding name - PFRQ27
    Information - injury prone
    Value labels -

        1.00   rarely to never
        2.00   sometimes
        3.00   frequently

FEMA Parent Fire Risk Questionnaire Variable 28

    Coding name - PFRQ28
    Information - shyness
    Value labels -

        1.00   rarely to never
        2.00   sometimes
        3.00   frequently

FEMA Parent Fire Risk Questionnaire Variable 29

    Coding name - PFRQ29
    Information - tries to please everyone
    Value labels -

        1.00   rarely to never
        2.00   sometimes
        3.00   frequently

FEMA Parent Fire Risk Questionnaire Variable 30

    Coding name - PFRQ30
    Information - relationships are socially appropriate
    Value labels -

        1.00   rarely to never
        2.00   sometimes
        3.00   frequently

FEMA Parent Fire Risk Questionnaire Variable 31

    Coding name - PFRQ31
    Information - physically fights with peers
    Value labels -

        1.00   rarely to never
        2.00   sometimes
        3.00   frequently

FEMA Parent Fire Risk Questionnaire Variable 32

    Coding name - PFRQ32
    Information - withdraws from peers/groups
    Value labels -

        1.00   rarely to never
        2.00   sometimes
        3.00   frequently

FEMA Parent Fire Risk Questionnaire Variable 33

    Coding name - PFRQ33
    Information - destroys toys/property of others
    Value labels -

        1.00   rarely to never
        2.00   sometimes
        3.00   frequently

FEMA Parent Fire Risk Questionnaire Variable 34

    Coding name - PFRQ34
    Information - is a poor loser
    Value labels -

        1.00   rarely to never
        2.00   sometimes
        3.00   frequently

FEMA Parent Fire Risk Questionnaire Variable 35

    Coding name - PFRQ35
    Information - shows off for peers
    Value labels -

        1.00   rarely to never
        2.00   sometimes
        3.00   frequently

FEMA Parent Fire Risk Questionnaire Variable 36

    Coding name - PFRQ36
    Information - easily led by peers
    Value labels -

        1.00   rarely to never
        2.00   sometimes
        3.00   frequently

FEMA Parent Fire Risk Questionnaire Variable 37

    Coding name - PFRQ37
    Information - plays with other children
    Value labels -

        1.00   rarely to never
        2.00   sometimes
        3.00   frequently

FEMA Parent Fire Risk Questionnaire Variable 38

    Coding name - PFRQ38
    Information - shows appropriate peer affection
    Value labels -

        1.00   rarely to never
        2.00   sometimes
        3.00   frequently

FEMA Parent Fire Risk Questionnaire Variable 39

    Coding name - PFRQ39
    Information - plays alone (not even with adults)
    Value labels -

        1.00   rarely to never
        2.00   sometimes
        3.00   frequently

FEMA Parent Fire Risk Questionnaire Variable 40

    Coding name - PFRQ40
    Information - picked on by peers
    Value labels -

        1.00   rarely to never
        2.00   sometimes
        3.00   frequently

FEMA Parent Fire Risk Questionnaire Variable 41

    Coding name - PFRQ41
    Information - has many friends
    Value labels -

        1.00   rarely to never
        2.00   sometimes
        3.00   frequently

FEMA Parent Fire Risk Questionnaire Variable 42

    Coding name - PFRQ42
    Information - participates in sports
    Value labels -

        1.00   rarely to never
        2.00   sometimes
        3.00   frequently

FEMA Parent Fire Risk Questionnaire Variable 43

    Coding name - PFRQ43
    Information - is a loner (few friends)
    Value labels -

        1.00   rarely to never
        2.00   sometimes
        3.00   frequently

FEMA Parent Fire Risk Questionnaire Variable 44

    Coding name - PFRQ44
    Information - excessive and uncontrolled verbal anger
    Value labels -

        1.00   rarely to never
        2.00   sometimes
        3.00   frequently

FEMA Parent Fire Risk Questionnaire Variable 45

    Coding name - PFRQ45
    Information - physically violent
    Value labels -

        1.00   rarely to never
        2.00   sometimes
        3.00   frequently

FEMA Parent Fire Risk Questionnaire Variable 46

    Coding name - PFRQ46
    Information - steals
    Value labels -

        1.00   rarely to never
        2.00   sometimes
        3.00   frequently

FEMA Parent Fire Risk Questionnaire Variable 47

    Coding name - PFRQ47
    Information - cruel to animals
    Value labels -

        1.00   rarely to never
        2.00   **sometimes**
        3.00   **frequently**

FEMA Parent Fire Risk Questionnaire Variable 48

   Coding name - PFRQ48
   Information - cruel to children
   Value labels -

      1.00   rarely to never
      2.00   sometimes
      3.00   frequently

FEMA Parent Fire Risk Questionnaire Variable 49

   Coding name - PFRQ49
   Information - is/was in a gang
   Value labels -

      1.00   rarely to never
      2.00   sometimes
      3.00   frequently

FEMA Parent Fire Risk Questionnaire Variable 50

   Coding name - PFRQ50
   Information - expresses anger by damaging the property of other
   Value labels -

      1.00   rarely to never
      2.00   sometimes
      3.00   frequently

FEMA Parent Fire Risk Questionnaire Variable 51

   Coding name - PFRQ51
   Information - destroys own toys/possessions (ages 3-6)
   Value labels -

      1.00   rarely to never
      2.00   sometimes
      3.00   frequently

FEMA Parent Fire Risk Questionnaire Variable 52

> Coding name - PFRQ52
> Information - destroys own possessions (ages 7-18)
> Value labels -
>
> > 1.00 rarely to never
> > 2.00 sometimes
> > 3.00 frequently

FEMA Parent Fire Risk Questionnaire Variable 53

> Coding name - PFRQ53
> Information - disobeys
> Value labels -
>
> > 1.00 rarely to never
> > 2.00 sometimes
> > 3.00 frequently

FEMA Parent Fire Risk Questionnaire Variable 54

> Coding name - PFRQ54
> Information - severe behavior difficulties (past or present)
> Value labels -
>
> > 1.00 rarely to never
> > 2.00 sometimes
> > 3.00 frequently

FEMA Parent Fire Risk Questionnaire Variable 55

> Coding name - PFRQ55
> Information - expresses anger by hurting others' things
> Value labels -
>
> > 1.00 rarely to never
> > 2.00 sometimes
> > 3.00 **frequently**

FEMA Parent Fire Risk Questionnaire Variable 56

    Coding name - PFRQ56
    Information - has been in trouble with police
    Value labels -

- 1.00 rarely to never
- 2.00 sometimes
- 3.00 frequently

FEMA Parent Fire Risk Questionnaire Variable 57

    Coding name - PFRQ57
    Information - uses drugs or alcohol
    Value labels -

- 1.00 rarely to never
- 2.00 sometimes
- 3.00 frequently

FEMA Parent Fire Risk Questionnaire Variable 58

    Coding name - PFRQ58
    Information - jealous of peers/siblings
    Value labels -

- 1.00 rarely to never
- 2.00 sometimes
- 3.00 frequently

FEMA Parent Fire Risk Questionnaire Variable 59

    Coding name - PFRQ59
    Information - temper tantrums
    Value labels -

- 1.00 rarely to never
- 2.00 sometimes
- 3.00 frequently

FEMA Parent Fire Risk Questionnaire Variable 60

    Coding name - PFRQ60
    Information - unacceptable showing off
    Value labels -

        1.00   rarely to never
        2.00   sometimes
        3.00   frequently

FEMA Parent Fire Risk Questionnaire Variable 61

    Coding name - PFRQ61
    Information - sexual activity with others
    Value labels -

        1.00   rarely to never
        2.00   sometimes
        3.00   frequently

FEMA Parent Fire Risk Questionnaire Variable 62

    Coding name - PFRQ62
    Information - lies
    Value labels -

        1.00   rarely to never
        2.00   sometimes
        3.00   frequently

FEMA Parent Fire Risk Questionnaire Variable 63

    Coding name - PFRQ63
    Information - stomach aches
    Value labels -

        1.00   rarely to never
        2.00   sometimes
        3.00   frequently

FEMA Parent Fire Risk Questionnaire Variable 64

    Coding name - PFRQ64
    Information - nightmares
    Value labels -

        1.00   rarely to never
        2.00   sometimes
        3.00   frequently

FEMA Parent Fire Risk Questionnaire Variable 65

    Coding name - PFRQ65
    Information - sleeps too deep or problems waking up
    Value labels -

        1.00   rarely to never
        2.00   sometimes
        3.00   frequently

FEMA Parent Fire Risk Questionnaire Variable 66

    Coding name - PFRQ66
    Information - anxiety (nervousness)
    Value labels -

        1.00   rarely to never
        2.00   sometimes
        3.00   frequently

FEMA Parent Fire Risk Questionnaire Variable 67

    Coding name - PFRQ67
    Information - has twitches (eyes, face, etc.)
    Value labels -

        1.00   rarely to never
        2.00   sometimes
        3.00   frequently

FEMA Parent Fire Risk Questionnaire Variable 68

    Coding name - PFRQ68
    Information - cries
    Value labels -

        1.00   rarely to never
        2.00   sometimes
        3.00   frequently

FEMA Parent Fire Risk Questionnaire Variable 69

    Coding name - PFRQ69
    Information - bites nails
    Value labels -

        1.00   rarely to never
        2.00   sometimes
        3.00   frequently

FEMA Parent Fire Risk Questionnaire Variable 70

    Coding name - PFRQ70
    Information - vomits
    Value labels -

        1.00   rarely to never
        2.00   sometimes
        3.00   frequently

FEMA Parent Fire Risk Questionnaire Variable 71

    Coding name - PFRQ71
    Information - aches and pains
    Value labels -

        1.00   rarely to never
        2.00   sometimes
        3.00   frequently

FEMA Parent Fire Risk Questionnaire Variable 72

    Coding name - PFRQ72
    Information - chews odd/unusual things
    Value labels -

        1.00   rarely to never
        2.00   sometimes
        3.00   frequently

FEMA Parent Fire Risk Questionnaire Variable 73

    Coding name - PFRQ73
    Information - extreme mood swings
    Value labels -

        1.00   rarely to never
        2.00   sometimes
        3.00   frequently

FEMA Parent Fire Risk Questionnaire Variable 74

    Coding name - PFRQ74
    Information - depressed mood or withdrawal
    Value labels -

        1.00   rarely to never
        2.00   sometimes
        3.00   frequently

FEMA Parent Fire Risk Questionnaire Variable 75

    Coding name - PFRQ75
    Information - constipation
    Value labels -

        1.00   rarely to never
        2.00   sometimes
        3.00   frequently

FEMA Parent Fire Risk Questionnaire Variable 76

    Coding name - PFRQ76
    Information - diarrhea
    Value labels -

        1.00   rarely to never
        2.00   sometimes
        3.00   frequently

FEMA Parent Fire Risk Questionnaire Variable 77

    Coding name - PFRQ77
    Information - unnecessary or excessive self-imposed diets
    Value labels -

        1.00   rarely to never
        2.00   sometimes
        3.00   frequently

FEMA Parent Fire Risk Questionnaire Variable 78

    Coding name - PFRQ78
    Information - sleep walking
    Value labels -

        1.00   rarely to never
        2.00   sometimes
        3.00   frequently

FEMA Parent Fire Risk Questionnaire Variable 79

    Coding name - PFRQ79
    Information - phobias
    Value labels -

        1.00   rarely to never
        2.00   sometimes
        3.00   frequently

FEMA Parent Fire Risk Questionnaire Variable 80

    Coding name - PFRQ80
    Information - general fears
    Value labels -

        1.00   rarely to never
        2.00   sometimes
        3.00   frequently

FEMA Parent Fire Risk Questionnaire Variable 81

    Coding name - PFRQ81
    Information - curiosity about fire
    Value labels -

        1.00   rarely to never
        2.00   sometimes
        3.00   frequently

FEMA Parent Fire Risk Questionnaire Variable 82

    Coding name - PFRQ82
    Information - plays with matches/lighters
    Value labels -

        1.00   rarely to never
        2.00   sometimes
        3.00   frequently

FEMA Parent Fire Risk Questionnaire Variable 83

    Coding name - PFRQ83
    Information - plays with fire (singeing/burning)
    Value labels -

        1.00   rarely to never
        2.00   sometimes
        3.00   frequently

FEMA Parent Fire Risk Questionnaire Variable 84

    Coding name - PFRQ84
    Information - was concerned when fire got out of control
    Value labels -

        1.00   rarely to never
        2.00   sometimes
        3.00   frequently

FEMA Parent Fire Risk Questionnaire Variable 85

    Coding name - PFRQ85
    Information - was proud/boastful regarding firesetting/firestart
    Value labels -

        1.00   rarely to never
        2.00   sometimes
        3.00   frequently

FEMA Parent Fire Risk Questionnaire Variable 86

    Coding name - PFRQ86
    Information - stares at fire for long periods (fire fascination)

    Value labels -

        1.00   rarely to never
        2.00   sometimes
        3.00   frequently

FEMA Parent Fire Risk Questionnaire Variable 87

    Coding name - PFR87
    Information - unusual look on child's face when he/she stares at fire(s)

    Value labels -

        1.00   rarely to never
        2.00   sometimes
        3.00   frequently

FEMA Parent Fire Risk Questionnaire Variable 88

    Coding name - PFRQ88
    Information - daydreams or talks about fire
    Value labels -

        1.00   rarely to never
        2.00   sometimes
        3.00   frequently

FEMA Parent Fire Risk Questionnaire Variable 89

    Coding name - PFRQ89
    Information - fear of fire
    Value labels -

        1.00   rarely to never
        2.00   sometimes
        3.00   frequently

FEMA Parent Fire Risk Questionnaire Variable 90

    Coding name - PFRQ90
    Information - other(s) in family set fire(s) (past or present)
    Value labels -

        1.00   rarely to never
        2.00   sometimes
        3.00   frequently

FEMA Parent Fire Risk Questionnaire Variable 91

    Coding name - PFRQ91
    Information - set occupied structure on fire (check one)
    Value labels -

        1.00   rarely to never
        2.00   sometimes
        3.00   frequently

FEMA Parent Fire Risk Questionnaire Variable 92

    Coding name - PFRQ92
    Information - appropriate reaction to fire(s) he/she set (check one)

    Value labels -

        1.00   rarely to never
        2.00   sometimes
        3.00   frequently

FEMA Parent Fire Risk Questionnaire Variable 93

    Coding name - PFRQ93
    Information - extensive absences by father
    Value labels -

        1.00   rarely to never
        2.00   sometimes
        3.00   frequently

FEMA Parent Fire Risk Questionnaire Variable 94

    Coding name - PFRQ94
    Information - extensive absences by mother
    Value labels -

        1.00   rarely to never
        2.00   sometimes
        3.00   frequently

FEMA Parent Fire Risk Questionnaire Variable 95

    Coding name - PFRQ95
    Information - family has moved
    Value labels -

        1.00   rarely to never
        2.00   sometimes
        3.00   frequently

FEMA Parent Fire Risk Questionnaire Variable 96

    Coding name - PFRQ96
    Information - runs away from home
    Value labels -

        1.00   rarely to never
        2.00   sometimes
        3.00   frequently

FEMA Parent Fire Risk Questionnaire Variable 97

    Coding name - PFRQ97
    Information - has seen a counselor/therapist
    Value labels -

        1.00   rarely to never
        2.00   sometimes
        3.00   frequently

FEMA Parent Fire Risk Questionnaire Variable 98

    Coding name - PFRQ98
    Information - other family member has seen a counselor/therapist

    Value labels -

        1.00   rarely to never
        2.00   sometimes
        3.00   frequently

FEMA Parent Fire Risk Questionnaire Variable 99

    Coding name - PFRQ99
    Information - makes attempts at age appropriate independence from parents

    Value labels -

        1.00   rarely to never
        2.00   sometimes
        3.00   frequently

FEMA Parent Fire Risk Questionnaire Variable 100

    Coding name - PFRQ100
    Information - in trouble at home
    Value labels -

        1.00   rarely to never
        2.00   sometimes
        3.00   frequently

FEMA Parent Fire Risk Questionnaire Variable 101

    Coding name - PFRQ101
    Information - parent or sibling with serious health problem

    Value labels -

        1.00   rarely to never
        2.00   sometimes
        3.00   frequently

FEMA Parent Fire Risk Questionnaire Variable 102

    Coding name - PFRQ102
    Information - marriage is unhappy
    Value labels -

        1.00   rarely to never
        2.00   sometimes
        3.00   frequently

FEMA Parent Fire Risk Questionnaire Variable 103

    Coding name - PFRQ103
    Information - female caregiver's discipline is effective
    Value labels -

        1.00   rarely to never
        2.00   sometimes
        3.00   frequently

FEMA Parent Fire Risk Questionnaire Variable 104

    Coding name - PFRQ104
    Information - male caregiver's discipline is effective
    Value labels -

        1.00   rarely to never
        2.00   sometimes
        3.00   frequently

FEMA Parent Fire Risk Questionnaire Variable 105

    Coding name - PFRQ105
    Information - fighting with siblings
    Value labels -

        1.00   rarely to never
        2.00   sometimes
        3.00   frequently

FEMA Parent Fire Risk Questionnaire Variable 106

    Coding name - PFRQ106
    Information - conflicts in family
    Value labels -

        1.00   rarely to never
        2.00   sometimes
        3.00   frequently

FEMA Parent Fire Risk Questionnaire Variable 107

    Coding name - PFRQ107
    Information - unusual fantasies
    Value labels -

        1.00   rarely to never
        2.00   sometimes
        3.00   frequently

FEMA Parent Fire Risk Questionnaire Variable 108

    Coding name - PFRQ108
    Information - strange thought patterns
    Value labels -

        1.00   rarely to never
        2.00   sometimes
        3.00   frequently

FEMA Parent Fire Risk Questionnaire Variable 109

    Coding name - PFRQ109
    Information - bizarre/illogical/irrational speech
    Value labels -

        1.00   rarely to never
        2.00   sometimes
        3.00   frequently

FEMA Parent Fire Risk Questionnaire Variable 110

    Coding name - PFRQ110
    Information - out of touch with reality
    Value labels -

        1.00   rarely to never
        2.00   sometimes
        3.00   frequently

FEMA Parent Fire Risk Questionnaire Variable 111

    Coding name - PFRQ111
    Information - strange quality about child
    Value labels -

        1.00   rarely to never
        2.00   sometimes
        3.00   frequently

FEMA Parent Fire Risk Questionnaire Variable 112

    Coding name - PFRQ112
    Information - expresses anger by hurting self or something he likes
    Value labels -

        1.00   rarely to never
        2.00   sometimes
        3.00   frequently

FEMA Parent Fire Risk Questionnaire Variable 113

    Coding name - PFRQ113
    Information - destroys own property
    Value labels -

        1.00   rarely to never
        2.00   sometimes
        3.00   frequently

FEMA Parent Fire Risk Questionnaire Variable 114

    Coding name - PFRQ114
    Information - was/is in a cult
    Value labels -

        1.00   rarely to never
        2.00   sometimes
        3.00   frequently

FEMA Parent Fire Risk Questionnaire Variable 115

    Coding name - PFRQ115
    Information - severe depression or withdrawal
    Value labels -

        1.00   rarely to never
        2.00   sometimes
        3.00   frequently

FEMA Parent Fire Risk Questionnaire Variable 116

    Coding name - PFRQ116
    Information - poor or no eye contact
    Value labels -

        1.00   rarely to never
        2.00   sometimes
        3.00   frequently

Destructiveness of second fire

    Coding name - SNDFIRE
    Information - destructiveness of second fire
    Value labels -

        1.00   mild
        2.00   moderate
        3.00   severe
        4.00   extreme

Age Group of Juvenile

    Coding name - AGEGROUP
    Information - grouping of participants based on age group

    Value labels -

        1.00   child
        2.00   child
        3.00   early adolescent
        4.00   late adolescent

Level of Aggression

    Coding name - AGGRESS
    Information - aggression score based on a range of 0 - 100

Level of Delinquency

    Coding name - DELINQUE
    Information - delinquency score based on a range of 0 - 100

Level of Acting Out

> Coding name - ACTOUT
> Information - acting out score based on a range of 0 – 100

Level of Delinquency

> Coding name - DELIN
> Information - delinquency score based on a range of 0 – 100

Level of Social skills

> Coding name - LEVSOC
> Information – social skills score based on a range of 0 - 100